Algerian Chronicles

Albert Camus

❧

Algerian
Chronicles

❧

TRANSLATED BY ARTHUR GOLDHAMMER

WITH AN
INTRODUCTION BY ALICE KAPLAN

The Belknap Press of Harvard University Press
Cambridge, Massachusetts
London, England
2013

LIBRARY OF CONGRESS CATALOGING-IN-PUBLICATION DATA
Camus, Albert, 1913–1960.
[Chroniques algériennes, 1939–1958. English]
Algerian chronicles / Albert Camus ; translated by Arthur
Goldhammer ; with an introduction by Alice Kaplan.
p. cm.
Originally published in French: Paris : Gallimard, 1958.
Includes bibliographical references and index.
ISBN 978-0-674-07258-9 (alk. paper)
1. Algeria—Politics and government—20th century.
2. Algeria—Social conditions—20th century.
3. Algeria—History—Revolution, 1954–1962.
I. Title.
DT295.C293 2013
965.04—dc23   2012036100

Contents

CONTENTS

Translator's Note

Algerian Chronicles is a moving record of Albert Camus's distress at his inability to alleviate the series of tragedies that befell his homeland, Algeria, over a period of 20 years, from 1939 to 1958. Camus collected these reactions to current events in a volume originally entitled *Actuelles III*. It would no doubt have saddened him to learn that the sources of his heartache—the difficulty of reconciling European and non-European cultures, the senseless recourse to violence, the fatal spiral of repression and terror—are once again matters "of actuality," lending prescience to his original title.

After listening to Camus lecture, the writer Julien Green described him in terms that one might apply to a secular saint: "There is in this man a probity so obvious that it inspires almost immediate respect in me. To put it plainly, he is not like the others." This quality of authenticity is unmistakable throughout the pieces collected here. Camus wrote as a moralist, in the noblest sense of the term. In fact, he was a moralist in two different senses. In the French sense, he was a worthy heir to La Rochefoucauld and La Bruyère, *moralistes* who exposed the hidden selfishness in ostensibly selfless action, the hypocrisy in what society, for reasons of its own, hypocritically honors as virtue. But he was also a moralist in the American sense, a writer of "jeremiads," which, as Sacvan Bercovitch revealed, are best understood as appeals to the fatherland to return to the high ideals that it has set for itself and from which it has strayed. Here, it is primarily this second type of moralism that is on display. Camus addresses France, his second home, which he believed had not, in its policies toward Algeria, remained true to the founding ideals of its republican tradition—liberty, equality, and fraternity—which for Camus were the political virtues par excellence.

In this respect, Camus was quintessentially French, but he saw himself not only as a Frenchman but also as a man of the Mediterranean, a spiritual heir of Saint Francis who, as Camus put it in an early manifesto on "Mediterranean culture" (included in the supplementary material to this volume), "turned Christianity from a religion of inner torment into a hymn to nature and naïve joy." But "nature and naïve joy" could not survive in the climate of "soulless violence" that descended on Algeria, the land of Camus's birth and the very root of his being. The pieces in this volume trace the increasing effect of this violence, not only on Camus's allegiances but on the language in which he expressed his and his homeland's suffering.

Abstraction was not Camus's natural element. In his early reportage, he indulges in a minimum of economic theorizing to set the stage for his narratives, but the force of his writing lies in his ability to make the reader feel what it is like to eat thistle, to depend on capricious handouts, or to die of exhaustion in the snow on the way home from a food distribution center. Although he may on occasion use an abstract and value-laden term like "justice," what moves him is plain fellow-feeling for other suffering human beings. With almost Franciscan faith he hopes that the example of his own compassion will suffice to elicit the compassion of others.

Attentive to Camus's text, the translator senses not only his despair of the situation in Algeria but also his exasperation. The political dilemmas of the time were cruel, and no *intellectuel engagé* escaped from them unscathed. History chose a course different from the one Camus envisioned, but history's choice has not been so incontrovertibly satisfactory as to rob Camus's counterfactual alternative of its retrospective grandeur. What we have here is a precious document of a soul's torment lived in real rather than eternal time. I can only hope that my translation has done it justice.

And it is not easy to do justice to Camus's style in English. He is a writer who has fully mastered all the resources of concision, subtlety, and grace that French provides. He can maintain perfect equipoise through a series of long sentences and then punctuate his point with a short phrase intensified by a slightly unusual syntax or surprising word choice. To mimic the French structure slavishly is to betray the spirit of the text, which has to be rethought with the different stylistic resources of English in mind. When I think of Camus's prose, I think of adjectives such as "pure," "restrained," and "disciplined." He never strains for effect, never descends into bathos, and always modulates his passion with classical precision.

When this book originally went to press, Camus was feeling desperate about Algeria's future, yet he concluded that it was still worth publishing the record of his own engagement, because of the facts it contained. "The facts have not changed," he wrote, "and someday these will have to be recognized if we are to achieve the only acceptable future: a future in which France, wholeheartedly embracing its tradition of liberty, does justice to all the communities of Algeria without discrimination in favor of one or another. Today as in the past, my only ambition in publishing this independent account is to contribute as best I can to defining that future." For us, half a century later, the facts still have not changed, and the future to which Camus hoped to contribute has expanded to include not just France but the entire world. Like Camus, we cannot change the obdurate facts of the past, but we can hope to learn from his unflinchingly honest account how better to deal with them in charting our own course.

—Arthur Goldhammer

Algerian Chronicles

New Perspectives on Camus's Algerian Chronicles

∾

ALICE KAPLAN

Albert Camus published his *Algerian Chronicles* on June 16, 1958, just as France was reeling from her greatest political upheaval since the end of the Second World War. The Fourth Republic had fallen, and when a coup d'état by rebellious French generals in Algeria seemed to be in the offing, General de Gaulle was called back to power to save the Republic. In the throes of a national crisis brought on wholly by the Algerian War, Camus gathered his writing on Algeria from 1939, when he was a political activist and an all-purpose reporter for *Alger républicain,* through the 1950s. He added an introduction and a concluding essay called "Algeria 1958." Yet his book was met, paradoxically, with widespread critical silence. The press file in the archives

I am grateful to P. Guillaume Michel at the Glycines: Centre d'Etudes Diocésain for his generous introduction to intellectual life in Algiers in the summer of 2012, and to the Algerian scholars who responded to my lecture on the *Chroniques algériennes* and opened my eyes to new readings of Camus in Algeria today. Comments by David Carroll, James Le Sueur, and Raymond Gay-Crosier on an earlier version of this preface were invaluable.

at Gallimard is practically empty—it seemed, on the Algerian question at least, that the French were no longer listening to Camus.

One exception was René Maran, the seventy-one-year-old black French writer from Guadeloupe who had won the Goncourt Prize in 1921 for *Batuala,* a colonial novel set in Africa. Maran believed that Camus's essays might one day seem as prescient of Algerian reality as Tocqueville's had been of life in Russia and the United States.[1] Reading the *Algerian Chronicles* for the first time in Arthur Goldhammer's elegant, concise translation, we might ask whether Maran was right.

———

The *Algerian Chronicles* have a double-edged message, as does so much of Camus's political writing. Throughout these essays spanning two decades of activism, he remains sensitive to the demands of the Algerian nationalists and their critique of colonial injustice. But an Algeria without the French is unimaginable to him, and he warns that a break with France will be fatal to any conceivable Algerian future.

Camus's position was appalling to many supporters of the Algerian cause, from the *porteurs de valises*—supporters of the Front de Libération Nationale who risked their own safety by carrying documents and money in support of the movement—to strictly intellectual critics of colonialism. He incurred the anger of the Algerian nationalists when he wrote that "to demand national independence for Algeria is a purely emotional response to the situation. There has never been an Algerian nation." Equally provocative, in the context of 1958, was his claim that the French in Algeria were, after

1. René Maran, "Chronique littéraire," *La Corrèze,* August 9, 1958.

130 years of colonization, "an indigenous population in the full sense of the word."

It's important to say what *Algerian Chronicles* is not. Camus does not take on the structures of colonial domination. Among his contemporaries, Sartre, in "Colonialism Is a System" (*Situations*, 1956) gives the classic economic analysis, and Albert Memmi in *The Colonizer and the Colonized* (1957), the psychological diagnosis.[2] Camus hoped that equal treatment could unite all the peoples of Algeria, and he believed that equality and justice would be enough to break the cycle of poverty and violence. He endorsed a federated Algeria where Berbers, Arabs, Jews, and Europeans could live together. Diagnosed with tuberculosis at age 17, with recurrent relapses, Camus felt the hopelessness of that solution in his very breath. As his hopes were dashed, he wrote to a moderate nationalist, Aziz Kessous, with a reference to the tuberculosis that had beset him for so many years: "Believe me when I tell you that Algeria is where I hurt at this moment, as others feel pain in their lungs."

———

Albert Camus was born in Mondovi in 1913 to a mother of Spanish origins who was both deaf and illiterate. His father died in the Battle of the Marne when Camus was barely a year old. Young Camus grew up in a three-room apartment in the working-class Belcourt neighborhood of Algiers with his domineering grandmother, his silent mother, who supported the family by cleaning houses, his brother Lucien, and his uncle Etienne, a barrel maker. A grade school teacher, Louis Germain, recognized his talent and

2. Jean-Paul Sartre, "Colonialism Is a System," in *Colonialism and Neocolonialism* (New York: Routledge, 2001), 30–47; Albert Memmi, *The Colonizer and the Colonized* (Boston: Beacon Press, 1991).

saw him through to the lycée, and after completing his under-graduate studies in philosophy at the University of Algiers, with a thesis on Plotinus and Saint Augustine, he turned to theater, to journalism, and to the literary career that led him to Paris, the anti-Nazi resistance, and the many books we know, until his life was cut short by a car accident in 1960, when he was forty-six years old. Long after Camus left Algeria, his writing remained imbued with his intense love of Algerian landscapes—the mountainous Kabylia, the Roman ruins of coastal Tipasa, the shining port of Algiers, and the modest blue balcony of his mother's apartment on the rue de Lyon. Those places were his wellspring.

But by the time *Algerian Chronicles* appeared, Camus was out of touch with the political and social realities of a country where, aside from brief stays, he hadn't lived since 1942. In 1956, he traveled to Algiers for a last-ditch political effort. No longer the poor schoolboy in Belcourt, the now renowned writer was staying at the luxurious Hôtel Saint-Georges high up in the city, drafting his "Call for a Civilian Truce." A roundtable was organized at the Cercle du Progrès that would bring together representatives of various political and religious groups who might be in a position to impose a civilian truce in a country being torn apart by terrorism from the French army, on the one hand, and the dominant Front de Libération Nationale, on the other. At the meeting was Doctor Khaldi from the Muslim community, Ferhat Abbas from the moderate Party of the Manifesto (Abbas would soon join the FLN), and representatives from the Catholic and Protestant churches in Algeria. Camus's frustration was palpable in his speech: "If I had the power to give voice to the solitude and distress that each of us feels, I would speak to you in that voice." He heard the French "ultracolonialists" in the crowd shouting "Death to Camus!" but he didn't know that he was under the protection of the Front de Libération Nationale that day—the same FLN he decries in his foreword to *Algerian Chronicles* for their murderous violence toward French and Arabs alike, and who would emerge to lead the first free Algeria in 1962. Roger Grenier has emphasized how much the writer was out of sync that day: "For the European liberals, the civilian truce was the last hope. For the Islamic nationalists—though they hid this carefully—it was merely a strategic maneuver."[3] Camus's moment of solitude was, for so many others, a high moment of revolutionary fervor.

Camus frames the *Algerian Chronicles* with references to his silence. After his coalition failed to achieve a civilian truce, Camus refused to make a public statement on the Algerian question, convinced that whatever he might say could only exacerbate the conflict by provoking the rage of one side or the other. *Algerian Chronicles* is his very public way of breaking his silence, his last hope to have some influence, and it was certainly another blow to him that nobody seemed to be listening. The book ends with the dramatic promise of "the last warning that can be given by a writer . . . before he lapses once again into silence."

It's not unusual to find, in the years following his death and still today, polemics that chastise him for not signing the Manifesto for the 121, a petition of leading French intellectuals calling for military insubordination by Algerian war draftees.[4] The manifesto was published, and promptly censored, nine months after Camus's death. His 29-month silence, from January 1956 to June 1958, became a metonymy for cowardice. And of course, his actual death in 1960 made that 29-month silence permanent. It's worth

---

3. Roger Grenier, *Albert Camus: Soleil et ombre* (Paris: Gallimard, 1987), 306.
4. See for example Susan Sontag, "The Ideal Husband," *New York Review of Books,* September 26, 1963, reviewing a translation of Camus's *Notebooks* from 1935 to 1942.

emphasizing that Camus was no longer alive when Francis Jeanson's network was put on trial for its support of the FLN, nor when the 121 intellectuals signed their manifesto, nor when Sartre prefaced Fanon's *The Wretched of the Earth,* nor, indeed, when the war ended with the Evian Accords in 1962. It's impossible to know exactly how Camus might have reacted to those events.

Camus's 1957 collection of short stories, *Exile and the Kingdom,* includes a short story about politics and silence called "Les Muets"— literally "The Mutes," but usually translated as "The Silent Men." Silence was fundamental to Camus, through his love for his deaf-mute mother. In a way you could even say that silence, not French, was this writer's mother tongue. In "The Silent Men," a workshop of barrel makers, a half-dozen Frenchmen and a single Arab, go out on strike for better wages. Management won't budge, and the union sends them all back to work, having negotiated a pitiful agreement that gives them the right to earn back wages by working overtime. Their amicable French boss, who has always treated them with paternalistic bonhomie, now comes to greet them as if nothing has changed. They respond with silence, and when he insists, more silence. There was no concerted plan among them to say nothing; it was spontaneous, a collective imperative, and the narrator of the story, trying to understand, concludes that "anger and helplessness sometimes hurt so much that you can't even cry out." Giving speech to anger and helplessness and injustice is the task Camus set for himself in publishing the *Algerian Chronicles.* His sense of impending loss, his horror of terror, even his vacillations, endow the book with many moments of literary beauty, and with an uncanny relevance.

———

If until recently *Algerian Chronicles* has been somewhat forgotten in France, the book's legacy in the United States and England is even more obscure. This is the only work by Camus never to have been published in its entirety in English translation.

Instead of *Algerian Chronicles,* Knopf and Hamish Hamilton published *Resistance, Rebellion, and Death* in 1961. In the last year of his life, Camus had prepared a selection of newspaper articles, speeches, and position papers spanning his entire career. He selected his "Letter to a German Friend" from 1944, a few of his articles in *Combat* on the Liberation of Paris, a text on Spain and on the Hungarian insurrection of 1956, his *Reflections on the Guillotine,* and less than a quarter of the full text of *Algerian Chronicles.* Arthur Goldhammer has done a great service in his retranslation of the previously translated pieces as well as the new material, bringing Camus's language into clear focus.[5]

Resistance, Rebellion, and Death was a good title for an English-speaking public in 1961, who understood Camus in abstract, not specific terms. The average reader of Camus in the United States and England may not even have known that Camus and Sartre disagreed violently on whether Algeria should be independent, nor that they had fallen out over their political differences. Camus was still largely identified in the public mind with his resistance to Nazism during the Occupation, and with his first novels. Titles go in and out of fashion like everything else, and Camus imposed short, essential titles that exuded metaphysical intensity: *The Fall, The Plague, The Stranger, Exile and the Kingdom.* Hence, *Resistance, Rebellion, and Death:* "Resistance," to remind the reader of the

---

5. To take just one example, Camus's characteristic expression of political feeling through his own body is almost impossible to understand in *Resistance, Rebellion, and Death:* "Believe me when I tell you that Algeria is the cause of my suffering at present as others might say their chest is the cause of their suffering." The original French is beautiful: "Car vous me croirez sans peine si je vous dis que j'ai mal à l'Algérie, en ce moment, comme d'autres ont mal aux poumons." Goldhammer's version is clear: "Believe me when I tell you that Algeria is where I hurt at this moment, as others feel pain in their lungs."

writer's role in World War II; "Rebellion," to echo Camus's 1951 essay *The Rebel*; and "Death," referring to Camus's opposition to the death penalty—and to the fact of Camus's own death. The writer had passed quickly from life into legend.

———

In response to the generation of 1961, who tended to appreciate Camus in philosophical terms, classifying him with Sartre and Beauvoir and Malraux, a new generation of critics writing after the 1970s took their distance from the romance of existentialism. They confronted Camus with his Algerian origins and expressed their dissatisfaction. The Arabs of *La Peste* and *L'Etranger,* complained Edward Said, are "nameless beings used as background for the portentous European metaphysics explored by Camus."[6] The questions raised by this first generation of postcolonial literary critics still animate many a classroom debate: Why doesn't Meursault's Arab victim speak? (All we hear is another Arab playing on a little reed.) Why does the setting for *The Plague* look more like Marseille than Oran?

In 1994, the long-delayed publication of Camus's unfinished novel, *The First Man,* answered some of these questions, and rereading this novel today in tandem with *Algerian Chronicles* gives an even fuller picture of Camus's attitudes. The adult Jacques, who returns to his boyhood home in the midst of the Algerian war, helps an Arab escape the neighborhood lest he be blamed for a terrorist bombing: "'He hasn't done anything,' Jacques said. And the worker said, 'We should kill them all.'"

6. Edward Said, "Representing the Colonized: Anthropology's Interlocutors," *Critical Inquiry* 15, no. 2 (Winter 1989): 223. See his differently nuanced focus on Camus's despair in *Culture and Imperialism* (New York: Knopf, 1993), 185: Camus's work expresses "a waste and sadness we have still not completely understood or recovered from."

Jacques explains the difference between Arabs, French bosses, and "bandits" (terrorists) to his illiterate uncle Etienne/Ernest, the barrel maker, who tells him that the bosses are too tough, but the terrorists are impossible. In a chapter called "Mondoví," Camus describes a timeless bond between Arab and European farmers, destined to live together. And in his notes for the novel, he writes, in a much-debated fragment: "Return the land. Give all the land to the poor . . . the immense herd of the wretched, mostly Arab and a few French, and who live and survive here through stubbornness and endurance."[7]

———

Dismissed or disdained in 1958, *Algerian Chronicles* has a new life in 2013, a half-century after the independence Camus so feared. The book's critique of the dead end of terrorism—the word appears repeatedly, with respect to both sides of the conflict—its insistence on a multiplicity of cultures; its resistance to fundamentalisms, are as meaningful in contemporary Algeria as in London or New York. Camus's refusal of violence speaks to Algerians still recovering from the civil war of the 1990s—"the dirty wars," or "black decade" that resulted in an estimated 100,000 civilian deaths. The tragedy began in 1991, after an Islamic party emerged victorious in legislative elections and the government scuttled the electoral process to prevent a fundamentalist takeover. The army entered into conflict with the fighting arm of the Front Islamique du Salut. Massacres broke out throughout the country, and the chaos was so great that no one knew who was responsible. Murders were committed by the army and by the Islamic Front, and the army disguised its own violence to make the Islamists look

7. Albert Camus, *The First Man* (New York: Random House, 1995), 75, 176–97, 318.

worse. Hundreds of intellectuals, artists, and teachers were murdered; many others were forced into exile.

On a recent trip to Algiers, I discussed Camus's *Algerian Chronicles* with several Algerian professors of literature. They responded
by connecting Camus's distant positions first to the dirty wars of
the 1990s, and second to the revolutionary struggle of the 1950s.
In the 1990s, explained N——,

> A lot of Algerians realized that there might be a parallel, that
> they had become a little like those French Algerians from
> before, from the 1950s and '60s—Algerians whose stature as
> Algerians wasn't being recognized. Those Algerians in the
> 1990s recognized themselves in Camus—whose Algerian di-
> mension was denied, whether it was in his novels, in his re-
> fusal to take a position, or in the positions he did take—the
> constant vacillation, the hesitation, the not being able to fig-
> ure out what is going on or take a clear position. I remember
> how we felt threatened in our Algerian identity: what, we
> were supposed to leave Algeria now? We're as much Algeri-
> ans as they are! It was a scandal! Also there was the question
> of exile: people were leaving the country and they were criti-
> cized. Had they done the right thing? Did they have a choice?
> And so they started to reread Camus from that perspective.

A colleague objected. As she saw it, Camus was being rehabili-
tated as part of a revisionist history that considered the FLN
guilty of acts of violence equal to French colonial violence. That
revisionism was erasing the just cause for which they had fought.

Both agreed that Camus had been unwelcome in the Algerian
classroom for a long time, and the decision in the 1980s to make
Arabic the obligatory language in the universities had put yet

another nail in his coffin. With French reduced to a second language, Camus had no official place in the national canon. He was, as N—— said, denied his Algerian-ness, now in literary terms. N—— pointed out that the founding fathers of Algerian national literature—Mohammed Dib, Maloud Feraoun, Kateb Yacine— were in literary dialogue with Camus, so that it was difficult to teach them without also teaching him. Yacine's national epic, *Nedjma* (1956), starts with a knife that recalls the knife carried by the Arab in *The Stranger*, only now it's not a European killing an Arab, but an Algerian worker attacking his European foreman. The Kabyle writer Maloud Feraoun, assassinated in 1962, uses an epigraph from *The Plague* in his first published novel, *The Poor Man's Son* (1950): "In man, there is far more to admire than to despise."[8] These writers were angry with Camus, or disappointed in him. But they remained in conversation with him. "A quarrel," as Sartre said about his own break with Camus, "is just another way of living together."

And so the conversation continues. Nabil, the narrator of Hamid Grine's 2011 novel *Camus dans le narguilé* (Camus in the hookah), buries his father and learns from an uncle at the funeral that his real, biological father is Albert Camus. He begins a quest that is also an allegory, with Camus as a stand-in for a lost literary heritage. As Algeria changes, the imaginary conversation with the figure of Camus changes, too.[9]

8. The epigraph is to an epilogue to the first 1950 edition of the novel; a subsequent 1954 edition has no epilogue, but the original edition has been translated as *The Poor Man's Son: Menrad, Kabyle Schoolteacher* (Charlottesville: University of Virginia Press, 2005). James Le Sueur's introduction explains the novel's complex history.

9. Hamid Grine, *Camus dans le narguilé* (Paris: Editions Après la Lune, 2011). Among Algerian writers and critics who have published influential work on Camus: Maïssa Bey, *L'ombre d'un homme qui marche au soleil: Réflexions sur Albert Camus* (Montpellier: Editions Chèvre-Feuille Etoilée, 2006), and two collections edited by Aïcha Kassoul and

Perhaps no Algerian writer has given more retrospective power to Camus than Assia Djebar, who has lived in exile in France and the United States since 1980. In her *Algerian White: A Narrative*, she compares Camus to Nelson Mandela.[10] She argues that the meeting for a civilian truce was the key moment when everything might have happened differently, and without violence, for Algeria. It's as if she were remembering that memorable moment in *The Stranger*, just as Meursault is about to fire on the Arab: "and there, in that noise, sharp and deafening at the same time, is where it all started. . . . And it was like knocking four quick times on the door of unhappiness."[11] Djebar makes a similar gesture, a writer's gesture. Of course there was no single moment, but she wants us to imagine that there was, in fact, one decisive moment—when leaders, French and Algerian, could either end the violence, or enable it. "People expect too much of writers in these matters," Camus might have said.[12]

Some Algerians thought, by 2010, that Camus had returned to favor. There was a plan for a Camus caravan to travel through the country giving readings. But it was canceled, for reasons no one could explain.

———

Camus's investigative pieces on Kabylia from *Algerian Chronicles* were not included in *Resistance, Rebellion, and Death*, perhaps because they don't match that book's philosophical themes, or per-

---

Mohamed Lakhdar Maougal, *Albert Camus: Assassinat Post-Mortem* (Alger: Editions APIC, 2005), and *Albert Camus et le choc des civilizations* (Alger: Editions Mille Feuilles, 2009).

10. Assia Djebar, *Algerian White: A Narrative* (New York: Seven Stories Press, 2000), 109.

11. Albert Camus, *The Stranger* (1942), trans. Matthew Ward (New York: Random House/Vintage, 1989), 59.

12. From the preface to *Algerian Chronicles*.

haps because they are full of details of French governance in a far-flung, mountainous region of Algeria that was completely unfamiliar to 1960s readers in the United States and Britain. In 1939, accompanied by a photographer, Camus traveled to Kabylia to write a series of reports for the anticolonialist *Alger républicain*, a newspaper that ran on a shoestring but gave the young writer the chance to report on everything from murder trials to books and plays. Two decades later, when he sat down to write a short story about a schoolteacher in mountainous Algeria, he used famine-stricken Kabylia as his backdrop. "The Guest"—"L'Hôte" in French, which can mean either "guest" or "host"—was published in *Exile and the Kingdom* in 1957. You find in it the French-run local government, the imported sacks of grain, the drought: "But it would be hard to forget that poverty, that army of ragged ghosts wandering in the sunlight," says the narrator, and actually, it's Camus's memory of his 1939 trip that is unforgettable.[13] "The Misery of Kabylia" is better documented than any other essay in *Algerian Chronicles*: Camus reviews the statistics on food supplies, nutrition, famine, and education. At least one of his suggestions—that impoverished Kabyles could improve their lot by leaving to work in mainland France—is shocking to Algerian readers today. But he is deeply informed and angry at a time when other journalists in France took any complaint about Algerian poverty as an attack on French values. "The Misery of Kabylia" is also in some ways the most literary piece in the *Chronicles*. There are moments of tragic contemplation, such as this scene with a Kabylian friend, looking over Tizi-Ouzou from the heights of the city at nightfall:

13. "Greece in rags" is the title of one of the articles in the series that Camus did not reprint in the *Chronicles*: "La Grèce en haillons," in *Oeuvres complètes*, ed. Jacqueline Lévi-Valensi (Paris: Gallimard, Bibliothèque de la Pléiade, 2006), 1:653–56.

And at that hour, when the shadows descending from the mountains across this splendid land can soften even the hardest of hearts, I knew that there was no peace for those who, on the other side of the valley, were gathering around a spoiled barleycake. I also knew that while it would have been comforting to surrender to the startling grandeur of that night, the misery gathered around the glowing fires across the way placed the beauty of this world under a kind of ban.

"Let's go down now, shall we?" my friend said.

In Kabylia, beauty and poverty exist together, but to sense them both is intolerable.

"The Misery of Kabylia" may seem gently humanitarian today, but in 1939 it contributed to the shutting down of Camus's newspaper and to his blacklisting by the French government in Algeria. He was unable to find a job with any newspaper and was forced to leave the country. This was his first exile. For the rest of his life, he believed he had risked everything for his anticolonial activism. After the war, in 1945, his articles in *Combat* represented a unique understanding of the riots at Sétif—that rally of Algerian veterans that led to a hundred European deaths and then to many thousands of Muslim deaths in the government repression that followed.[14] While Camus understood the political implications of Sétif, the communist press referred to the rioters as "fas-

14. "European" and "Muslim" have never been mutually exclusive terms, but in pre-independence Algeria they served to distinguish colonizers and settlers of European origin from indigenous Arab and Berber populations living under French rule.

cist *agents provocateurs.*"[15] Camus was convinced that if the French government continued to ignore poverty and famine in Algeria, if it continued to pursue its violent colonization and reinforce discrimination against native-born Algerians, France would and should lose Algeria. By the late 1950s, he found himself in a position that was incomprehensible to him: censured by the very cause he had so ardently defended and reduced, because of his opposition to the FLN, to an enemy of Algeria. He made fun, in turn, of the French who had only recently "discovered" the Algerian cause: "If you read certain newspapers, you get the impression that Algeria is a land of a million whip-wielding, cigar-chomping colonists driving around in Cadillacs."

────────

Camus's state of mind in 1958 dominates most discussions of his relationship to Algeria, drowning out the rest. But it's important to understand how his position evolved from his earliest anti-colonialist activism. In addition to the never-before-translated "The Misery of Kabylia," this Harvard edition of *Algerian Chronicles* includes an appendix of lesser-known texts that did not appear in the French edition of 1958. They add to our sense of Camus's specific commitments in Algeria and show him acting on those commitments. "Indigenous Culture: The New Mediterranean Culture" is a lecture from 1937, when Camus ran a Communist Party cultural center in Algiers. Here he wrests the meaning of Mediterranean culture from the right-wing and racialized

15. See *L'Humanité,* May 11 and June 30, 1945, as well as the analysis by Alain Ruscio, "Les Communistes et les massacres du Constantinois (mai–juin 1945)," *Vingtième siècle: Revue d'histoire* 94 (April–June 2007): 217–29.

notion of the "Latin genius" that was central to the ideology of Charles Maurras's Action Française.

There is an eccentric, but significant Algerian text included here, a micro-narrative: in a 1938 newspaper article, "Men Stricken from the Rolls of Humanity," Camus describes prisoners caged in the hold of a ship in the port of Algiers before being sent to the penal colonies. Camus boards the ship and passes an Algerian prisoner who is clutching the bars of his cage. The man asks him for a cigarette. I believe it's the only place in all of Camus's work where the writer shows that he hears, and understands, if only the simplest sentence in Arabic.

There is a letter to the editor of the French daily *Le Monde* in response to police violence against North Africans on July 14, 1953, in Paris. The police fired on demonstrators who were protesting the arrest of Messali Hadj, leader of an early independence movement. There were seven deaths and a hundred people wounded. For Camus, the police violence was motivated by racism: "one is justified, I think, in asking whether the press, the government, and Parliament would have been quite so nonchalant if the demonstrators had not been North Africans, and whether the police would have fired with such confident abandon."

We also include here the full draft of a letter that appeared in an abridged version, in English, in a 1957 issue of the British magazine *Encounter*—a rare statement, perhaps the only one—published anywhere during Camus's self-imposed "silent period." The writer addresses the charge that he argued for Hungarian freedom from the Soviets yet wouldn't support the same freedom for Algerians. The shortened letter published in *Encounter* synthesizes his position: "The Hungarian problem is simple: the Hungarians must have their freedom back. The Algerian problem is different: the freedoms of two groups of people must be guaranteed."[16]

Finally, among the most interesting documents to come to light in recent years are two of Camus's private letters to the French president René Coty, protesting death sentences imposed on Algerian freedom fighters—members of the same Front de Libération Nationale whose tactics he deplored. These letters were discovered by Eve Morisi in the Camus archives in Aix-en-Provence.[17] When, on the occasion of his Nobel Prize, Camus told an Algerian student at a press conference in Stockholm that he had done more for the Algerian cause than the young man could know, he was certainly thinking about these private letters:

> As an Algerian-born Frenchman whose entire family lives in Algiers and who is aware of the threat that terrorism poses to my own kin as to all the inhabitants of Algeria, I am affected daily by the current tragedy, and deeply enough that, as a writer and journalist, I have resolved to take no public step that might, despite the best intentions in the world, aggravate rather than improve the situation.

Germaine Tillion estimated that Camus intervened in over 150 cases.[18]

When Camus spoke in Stockholm about the men whose lives he had saved behind the scenes, he may have been overly optimistic: four of the ten condemned men he named in a footnote to his September 1957 letter to the French president were guillotined a

---

16. Camus's published letter can be found in the letters section of the June 1957 issue of *Encounter*, 68.

17. See Eve Morisi, ed., *Camus contre la peine de mort* (Paris: Gallimard, 2011).

18. Olivier Todd, *Albert Camus: A Life* (New York: Knopf, 1997), 399.

month later. Today in Algiers, the names of all the guillotined men from the Algerian War are inscribed, in Arabic, outside the former Barberousse prison.

Finally we include the polemic around Camus's 1957 Stockholm press conference with its tragicomedy of misquotation. When the Algerian student arguing the cause of the FLN challenged Camus, the Nobel laureate responded at length, ending with his infamous quid pro quo: "People are now planting bombs in the tramways of Algiers. My mother might be on one of those tramways. If that is justice, then I prefer my mother." *Le Monde* reported the sentence as "I believe in justice, but I will defend my mother before justice." It has often been reduced to a formula that makes Camus sound even more like a sentimental egoist: "Between justice and my mother, I choose my mother."[19] Three days after the press conference, he sent a letter of clarification to the director of *Le Monde*. With its gesture of unhappy empathy, its sympathy for the young Algerian nationalists, the letter explains, in a single phrase, the emotional conundrum that would move Camus, six months later, to publish his *Algerian Chronicles*: "I would also like to say, in regard to the young Algerian who questioned me, that I feel closer to him than to many French people who speak about Algeria without knowing it. He knew what he was talking about, and his face reflected not hatred but despair and unhappiness. I share that unhappiness."

19. Here is the sequence of sentences in the original French: "En ce moment on lance des bombes dans les tramways d'Alger. Ma mère peut se trouver dans un de ces tramways. Si c'est cela la justice, je préfère ma mère"; which became: "Je crois à la justice, mais je défendrai ma mère avant la justice"; which became "Entre la justice et ma mère, je choisis ma mère."

Algerian Chronicles

This volume had already been set in type and was about to appear when the events of May 13 occurred.[1] After giving some thought to the matter, I decided that it was still worth publishing, indeed, that it was in a way a direct commentary on these events, and that given the current confusion, the positions and possible solutions set forth here deserved more than ever to be heard. Minds in Algeria have changed a lot, and these changes arouse great hopes as well as great fears. But the facts have not changed, and someday these will have to be recognized if we are to achieve the only acceptable future: a future in which France, wholeheartedly embracing its tradition of liberty, does justice to all the communities of Algeria without discrimination in favor of one or another. Today as in the past, my only ambition in publishing this independent account is to contribute as best I can to defining that future.

---

1. On May 13, 1958, an insurrection of French settlers began in Algeria. Eventually this uprising led to General de Gaulle's return to power and, much to the dismay of the insurrectionists, ultimate independence for Algeria.

Preface

This book is a selection of articles about Algeria. They cover a period of 20 years, from 1939, when almost no one in France was interested in the country, to 1958, when everyone is talking about it. A single volume would not have been enough to contain these articles as originally written. Repetitions had to be eliminated, overly general commentary had to be compressed, and, above all, facts, figures, and suggestions that might still be useful had to be identified and retained. These texts summarize the position of a man who, having confronted the Algerian plight from the time he was very young, tried in vain to sound the alarm and who, being long aware of France's responsibility in the matter, could not approve of either a conservative or an oppressive policy. Owing to long familiarity with Algerian realities, however, I also cannot approve of a policy of surrender, which would abandon the Arab people to even greater misery, tear the French people of Algeria from their century-old roots, and do nothing but encourage the new imperialism that threatens the liberty of France and the West, to no one's benefit.

In the present situation, such a position will satisfy no one, and I know in advance how it will be received by both sides. I am sincerely sorry about this, but I cannot force myself to feel or believe what I do not. By the same token, no one else speaking out on the subject satisfies me either. That is why, finding it impossible to join either of the extreme camps, recognizing the gradual disappearance of the third camp in which it was still possible to keep a cool head, doubtful of my own certitudes and knowledge, and convinced that the true cause of our follies is to be found in the way in which our intellectual and political society habitually operates, I have decided to stop participating in the endless polemics whose only effect has been to make the contending factions in Algeria even more intransigent and to deepen the divisions in a France already poisoned by hatred and factionalism.

There is in fact a peculiar French nastiness, which I do not wish to compound. I am only too well aware of what this nastiness has cost us in the past and continues to cost us now. For the past 20 years, we have so detested our political adversaries that we have been prepared to accept anything else instead, including foreign dictatorship. The French apparently never tire of playing such lethal games. They are, as Custine observed, a singular people, who would rather flaunt their ugliness than be forgotten. If their country disappeared, however, it would be forgotten, no matter how it had been portrayed, and in an enslaved nation we would no longer have even the freedom to insult one another. Until these truths are recognized, we must resign ourselves to speaking only for ourselves, with all the necessary precautions. And speaking for myself, I must say that the only actions that interest me are those that can prevent, here and now, the pointless shedding of blood, and the only solutions that interest me are those that preserve the future of a world whose woes weigh on me too heavily to allow me to grandstand for the sake of the audience.

I have still other reasons for avoiding these public jousts. In the first place, I lack the assurance necessary to think I have all the answers. On this point, terrorism as practiced in Algeria has greatly influenced my attitude. When the fate of men and women who share one's own blood is linked directly or indirectly to articles that one writes so effortlessly in the comfort of one's study, then one has a duty to weigh the pros and cons before taking up one's pen. For my own part, while I remain sensitive to the risk that, in criticizing the course of the rebellion, I give aid and comfort to the most insolent instigators of the Algerian tragedy, I am also afraid that, by retracing the long history of French errors, I am, with no risk to myself, supplying alibis to the criminal madmen who would toss grenades into crowds of innocent people who happen to be my kin. Yet when I merely acknowledged this obvious fact in a recent statement, it drew some peculiar commentary. People who are unfamiliar with the situation I describe cannot readily judge it. As for those who are familiar with it yet continue to believe heroically that their brothers should die rather than their principles, I shall confine myself to admiring them from afar. I am not of their breed.

Not that those principles are meaningless. A conflict of ideas is possible, even between armed camps, and it is right to try to understand one's adversary's reasoning before defending oneself against him. But the use of terror as a tactic changes the priorities of both sides. When one's family is in immediate danger of death, one might wish that it were a more generous and just family and even feel obliged to make it so, as this book will attest, and yet (make no mistake!) remain in solidarity against the mortal threat, so that the family might at least survive and therefore preserve its opportunity to become more just. To my mind, this is what honor and true justice are—or, if not, then nothing I know is of any use in this world.

Only on this basis does one have the right and the duty to say that the armed struggle and repression that the French have undertaken are in some respects unacceptable. The reprisals against the civilian population of Algeria and the use of torture against the rebels are crimes for which we all bear a share of responsibility. That we have been able to do such things is a humiliating reality that we must henceforth face. Meanwhile, we must refuse to justify these methods on any grounds whatsoever, including effectiveness. Once one begins to justify them, even indirectly, no rules or values remain. One cause is as good as another, and pointless warfare, unrestrained by the rule of law, consecrates the triumph of nihilism. Whether intentionally or not, this takes us back to the law of the jungle, where violence is the only principle. Even those who have heard enough talk of morality must understand that even when it comes to winning wars, it is better to suffer certain injustices than to commit them, and that such actions do us more harm than a hundred enemy guerrillas. When, for example, these practices are used against those in Algeria who do not hesitate to massacre the innocent or torture or excuse torture, are they not also incalculable errors because they risk justifying the very crimes that we seek to fight? Can a method really be "effective" if its result is to justify the most unjustifiable actions of one's adversary? We must therefore confront head-on the most important argument advanced by those who have decided to use torture: it may have cost us something in the way of honor, they say, but it saved lives by leading to the discovery of 30 bombs. But it also created 50 new terrorists, who will employ different tactics in different places and cause the deaths of still more innocents. Even if dishonorable methods are accepted in the name of realism and effectiveness, they are therefore useless, except to discredit France both at home and abroad. Ultimately, these fine exploits will infallibly lead to the demoralization of France and the abandonment of Algeria. Censorship, which remains stupid whether imposed out of cynicism or shame, will not alter these basic truths. The government's duty is not to suppress protests against the criminal excesses of repression, even if the protesters are acting in the interest of one side in the conflict. It is rather to suppress the excesses themselves and to condemn them publicly, so as to avoid making every citizen feel personally responsible for the misdeeds of a few and therefore compelled either to denounce or defend them.

If, however, we wish to be useful as well as fair, we ought to condemn with equal force and in the bluntest of terms the terrorism practiced by the FLN[1] against French civilians and, even more frequently, Arab civilians. This terrorism is a crime, which can be neither excused nor allowed to develop. In the form in which it is currently practiced, no revolutionary movement has ever tolerated it, and the Russian terrorists of 1905 would sooner have died (as they proved) than stoop to such tactics. It is wrong to transform the injustices endured by the Arab people into a systematic indulgence of those who indiscriminately murder Arab and French civilians without regard to age or sex. After all, Gandhi proved that one could fight for one's people, and win, without forfeiting the world's esteem for an instant. No matter what cause one defends, it will suffer permanent disgrace if one resorts to blind attacks on crowds of innocent people in which the killer knows in advance that he will kill women and children.

As the reader will soon discover, I have said repeatedly that, if criticism is to be effective, both camps must be condemned. I therefore concluded that it was both indecent and harmful to denounce French torture in the company of critics who had nothing

---

1. The French abbreviation for National Liberation Front, the Algerian rebel organization.—*Trans.*

to say about Melouza[2] or the mutilation of European children. By the same token, I thought it harmful and indecent to condemn terrorism in the company of people whose consciences found torture easy to bear. The truth, unfortunately, is that one segment of French public opinion vaguely believes that the Arabs have somehow acquired the right to kill and mutilate, while another segment is prepared to justify every excess. Each side thus justifies its own actions by pointing to the crimes of its adversaries. This is a casuistry of blood with which intellectuals should, I think, have nothing to do, unless they are prepared to take up arms themselves. When violence answers violence in a mounting spiral, undermining the simple language of reason, the role of the intellectual cannot be to excuse the violence of one side and condemn that of the other, yet this is what we read every day. The effect of this is to further enrage the condemned party while inciting the exonerated perpetrator to even greater violence. If the intellectual does not join the combatants themselves, then his (admittedly less glorious) role must be simply to calm things down to the point where reason might again play its part. A perspicacious Right would therefore, without renouncing its convictions, have tried to persuade its supporters in Algeria and in the government of the need for deep reforms and of the dishonorable nature of certain methods. An intelligent Left, without sacrificing any of its principles, would have attempted to persuade the Arab movement that certain methods are inherently ignoble. But no. On the right, we hear France's honor repeatedly invoked to justify what is most damaging to that honor. On the left, we hear justice repeatedly cited as an excuse for

2. In 1957, 303 Muslim inhabits of the village of Melouza, or Mechtah-Kasbah, were killed by the FLN on the grounds that they supported a rival pro-independence group, the Mouvement National Algérien (MNA).—*Trans.*

affronts to any authentic idea of justice. The Right has thus ceded the moral response entirely to the Left, while the Left has ceded the patriotic response entirely to the Right. France has suffered from both reactions. The country needed moralists less joyfully resigned to their country's misfortune and patriots less willing to allow torturers to act in France's name. Metropolitan France has apparently been unable to come up with any political solution other than to say to the French of Algeria, "Die, you have it coming to you!" or "Kill them all, they've asked for it." Which makes for two different policies but one single surrender, because the real question is not how to die separately but how to live together.

I ask those who might be vexed by these words to set their ideological reflexes aside for a moment and just think. Some want their country to identify totally with justice, and they are right. But can one remain just and free in a nation that is defunct or enslaved? Is not absolute purity for a nation identical with historical death? Others want their country to be physically defended, against the entire world if need be, and they are not wrong. But can a people survive without being reasonably just toward other peoples? France is dying because it has not been able to resolve this dilemma. The first group of people wants the universal at the expense of the particular. The second wants the particular at the expense of the universal. But the two go together. Before we can discover human society, we must know national society. If national society is to be preserved, it must be open to a universal perspective. Specifically, if your goal is to have France rule alone over eight million silent subjects in Algeria, then France will die. If your goal is to sever Algeria from France, then both will perish. If, however, the French people and the Arab people unite their differences in Algeria, a meaningful future is possible for the French, the Arabs, and the entire world.

For that to happen, people must stop thinking of the Arabs of Algeria as a nation of butchers. The vast majority of them, exposed to blows from both sides, suffer in ways to which no one gives voice. Millions of them cower in fear and panic, yet neither Cairo nor Algiers speaks out in their behalf. As the reader will soon discover, I have long endeavored at least to make their misery known, and some will no doubt object to my somber descriptions of their plight. Yet I wrote these pleas on behalf of Arab misery when there was still time to act, at a time when France was strong and silence reigned among those who today find it easy to attack their enfeebled country, even on foreign soil. Had my voice been heard 20 years ago, there might be less bloodshed today. Unfortunately (and I experience it as a misfortune), events have proved me right. Today, the danger is that the poverty of the Algerian peasantry may grow rapidly worse as the population increases at a lightning pace. Caught between contending armies, these people are also afraid: they, too, need peace—they above all! I think of them as well as my own people whenever I write the word "Algeria" and plead for reconciliation. And it is they who must at last be given a voice and a future free of fear and hunger.

If that is to happen, though, there must also be an end to the wholesale condemnation of Algeria's French population. Some in France never tire of hating the French of Algeria unremittingly, and they must be recalled to decency. When a French supporter of the FLN dares to write that the French of Algeria have always looked upon France as a "prostitute" to be exploited, the irresponsible gentleman must be reminded that he is speaking of men and women whose grandparents opted for France in 1871 and left their native Alsace for Algeria; whose fathers died in great numbers in eastern France in 1914; and who, twice mobilized during the last war, joined hundreds of thousands of Muslims in the fight to defend that "prostitute" on all fronts. Knowing these things, one might still consider the French of Algeria naïve, but one can hardly accuse them of being "pimps." Here, I am recounting the story of my own family, which, being poor and devoid of hatred, never exploited or oppressed anyone. But three-quarters of the French in Algeria are like my relatives: if one provided them with reasons rather than insults, they would be prepared to admit the necessity of a more just and liberal order. There have of course been exploiters in Algeria, but far fewer than in the metropole, and the primary beneficiary of the colonial system has been the French nation as a whole. Even if there are Frenchmen who believe that France's colonial ventures have placed it (and it alone among nations otherwise holy and pure) in a historic state of sin, they need not offer up the French of Algeria as expiatory victims. They would do better to offer themselves up: "Die, all of us, we all have it coming!" The idea of acknowledging guilt as our judges-penitent do, by beating the breasts of others, revolts me. It is pointless to condemn several centuries of European expansion and absurd to curse Christopher Columbus and Marshal Lyautey in the same breath. The era of colonialism is over, and the only problem now is to draw the appropriate consequences. Furthermore, the West, which has granted independence to a dozen colonies over the past 10 years, deserves more respect and above all patience than Russia, which in the same period has colonized or placed under its implacable protection a dozen countries of great and ancient civilization. It is good for a nation to be strong enough in its traditions and honorable enough to find the courage to denounce its own errors, but it must not forget the reasons it may still have to think well of itself. It is in any case dangerous to ask it to confess sole responsibility and resign itself to perpetual penance. I believe in a policy of reparations for Algeria, not a policy of expiation. Issues must be raised with an eye to the future, without endless rehashing of past sins. And there will be no future that does not do justice to both communities in Algeria.

True, this spirit of fairness seems alien to the reality of our history, in which power relations have defined a different kind of justice. In our international society, the only morality is nuclear. Only the loser is culpable. It is easy to understand why many intellectuals have therefore concluded that values and words have no content but that with which they are invested by force. Some therefore move seamlessly from talk about principles of honor and fraternity to worship at the altar of the fait accompli or the cruelest party. I nevertheless continue to believe, about Algeria and everything else, that these errors of both the Right and the Left simply define the nihilism of our times. Although it is historically true that values such as the nation and humanity cannot survive unless one fights for them, fighting alone cannot justify them (nor can force). The fight must itself be justified, and explained, in terms of values. One must fight for one's truth while making sure not to kill that truth with the very arms employed to defend it: only if both criteria are satisfied can words recover their vital meaning. With this in mind, the role of the intellectual is to seek by his own lights to make out the respective limits of force and justice in each camp. It is to explain the meaning of words in such a way as to sober minds and calm fanaticisms, even if this means working against the grain.

I have tried to inject sobriety into the discussion. Admittedly, little has come of the effort so far. This book is among other things the history of a failure. But the simplifications of hatred and prejudice, which embitter and perpetuate the Algerian conflict, must be combated on a daily basis, and one man cannot do the job alone. What is required is a movement, a supportive press, and constant action. The lies and omissions that obscure the real problem must also be exposed on a daily basis. The government is already committed to undeclared war. It wants a free hand to deal with the problem as it sees fit while begging for money from our allies. It wants to invest in Algeria without jeopardizing the standard of living at home. It wants to be intransigent in public while negotiating in private. It wants to cover up the mistakes of its minions while quietly disavowing them. But the parties and factions that criticize the government are hardly shining examples either. What they want is never clearly stated, or, if it is, the consequences are not drawn. Those who favor a military solution must know that the methods of total war will be required, and this will also mean reconquering Tunisia against the wishes, and perhaps the weapons, of a part of the world. This is an option, to be sure, but it must be seen and presented for what it is. Those who advocate in deliberately vague terms negotiations with the FLN cannot be unaware that this would mean, according to the FLN's own statements, independence for Algeria under the rule of the most uncompromising leaders of the armed insurrection, and therefore the expulsion of 1.2 million Europeans from Algeria and the humiliation of millions of French citizens, with all the risks that such humiliation implies. This, too, is no doubt an option, but one must be candid about what it would mean and stop cloaking it in euphemisms.

It would mean engaging in constant polemic, which would be counterproductive in a society in which clear thinking and intellectual independence are increasingly rare. If you write a hundred articles, all that remains of them is the distorted interpretation imposed by your adversaries. A book may not avoid every possible misunderstanding, but it at least makes certain kinds of misunderstanding impossible. You can refer to the text, and you have more space to explain crucial nuances. Because I wanted to respond to the many people who have asked me in good faith to make my position clear, I therefore decided that the best way was to sum up 20 years' experience in this book, in the hope that those who wish to be enlightened might find something of value. I emphasize the word "experience," by which I mean a lengthy confrontation between a man and a situation—with all the errors, contradictions, and hesitations that such a confrontation implies, many examples of which can be found in the following pages. My opinion, moreover, is that people expect too much of writers in these matters. Even, and perhaps especially, when the writer is linked to the fate of a country like Algeria by birth and emotion, it is wrong to think that he is in possession of any revealed truth, and his personal history, were it possible to write such a history truthfully, is but a history of successive failures, of obstacles overcome only to be encountered yet again. On this point, I am quite ready to acknowledge the inadequacies and errors of judgment that readers may detect in these pages. Nevertheless, whatever the cost to me personally, I thought it might at least be possible to collect the many pieces I have written on this subject and lay them before people whose minds are not yet made up. The psychological détente that one senses right now between French and Arabs in Algeria also raises hopes that the language of reason might once again be heard.

In this book the reader will therefore find a discussion of the economic causes of the Algerian tragedy (in connection with a very serious crisis in Kabylia), some milestones in the political evolution of the crisis, comments on the complexity of the present situation, a prediction of the impasse to which the revival and repression of terrorism have led, and, finally, a brief sketch of what seems to me a still possible solution. Taking note of the end of colonialism, I rule out any thought of reconquest or continuation of the status quo, because these are really reactions of weakness and humiliation, which are laying the groundwork for an eventual divorce that will add to the woes of both France and Algeria. But I also rule out any thought of uprooting the French of Algeria, who do not have the right to oppress anyone but do have the right not to be oppressed themselves, as well as the right to determine their own future in the land of their birth. There are other ways to restore the justice that is indispensable than to replace one injustice by another.

I have tried to define my position clearly in this regard. An Algeria consisting of federated communities linked to France seems to me unquestionably preferable from the standpoint of justice to an Algeria linked to an Islamic empire that would subject the Arab peoples to additional misery and suffering and tear the French people of Algeria from their natural homeland. If the Algeria in which I invest my hopes still has any chance of coming into being (as I believe it does), then I want to help in any way I can. By contrast, I believe that I should not for one second or in any way help in the constitution of the other Algeria. If, contrary to French interests or remote from France, the forces of surrender were to converge with the forces of pure conservatism to consolidate a double defeat, I would feel immense sorrow, and along with millions of other Frenchmen I would have to draw the appropriate conclusions. That is my honest opinion. I may be mistaking or misjudging a tragedy that touches me personally. But if the hopes that one can today still reasonably entertain were to vanish tomorrow in the wake of grave events affecting our country or mankind as a whole, we will all be jointly responsible, and each of us will be accountable for what he or she has said and done. This is my testimony, and I shall have nothing more to say.

March–April 1958

THE MISERY OF KABYLIA

In early 1939, Kabylia suffered a cruel famine, whose causes and effects will be explored in this and subsequent articles. I was sent to the region as a reporter for *Alger républicain,* a daily newspaper that at the time had a Socialist and Radical coloration, and published these articles on June 5 and 15, 1939. The pieces were too long and detailed to reproduce here in their entirety, and I have cut overly general observations and sections on housing, welfare, crafts, and usury.

I

Destitution

Before attempting a broad overview of the misery in Kabylia and retracing the itinerary of famine that I have been following for many long days now, I want to say a few words about the economic causes of this misery. They can be summed up in one sentence: Kabylia is an overpopulated region that consumes more than it produces. These mountains enfold in their creases a teeming population, which in some villages, such as Djurdjura, attain a density of 247 inhabitants per square kilometer. No country in Europe is this crowded. The mean density in France is 71 per square kilometer. Furthermore, the Kabyle people consume mainly cereals such as wheat, barley, and sorghum in the form of flatcakes or couscous, but the Kabyle soil does not support these crops. The region's cereal production meets only one-eighth of its consumption needs. The grain necessary for life must therefore be purchased on the open market. In a region with virtually no industry, this can be done only by supplying a surplus of complementary agricultural produce.

Kabylia is mainly a country of orchards, however. Its two main cash crops are figs and olives. In many places, barely enough figs are produced to meet local consumption needs. Olive production varies from year to year: sometimes there is a shortfall, at other times an overabundance. How is the actual output to be kept in balance with the starving Kabyles' need for grain?

The Office of Wheat increased the price of that grain, and it had its reasons for doing so. But the price of figs and olives did not increase. The Kabyles, net importers of wheat, therefore paid the tribute of hunger to their splendid but harsh environment.

Like people in other poor, overpopulated regions of the world, the Kabyles responded to this difficult situation by emigrating. The facts are well-known. I will add only that the number of Kabyles living outside the region is estimated to be 40,000 to 50,000 and that in good times, the single district of Tizi-Ouzou was taking in as much as 40 million francs in remittances every month, while the commune of Fort-National received nearly a million a day. This enormous influx of capital, the product of Kabyle labor abroad, was enough to finance Kabylia's trade deficit in 1926. The region was then prosperous, and through tenacity and hard work the Kabyles managed to cope with poverty.

When the Depression came, however, the French labor market dried up. Kabyle workers were sent home. Immigration barriers were erected, and in 1935 a series of administrative orders complicated the procedures for entering France to the point where Kabyles felt imprisoned in their mountainous redoubt. Emigration was effectively blocked by requiring a payment of 165 francs for "repatriation fees" along with countless other administrative hurdles, as well as the unusual requirement that every would-be émigré pay any back taxes owed by compatriots with the same last name. To cite only one figure to illustrate the consequences of these new rules, the commune of Michelet received only one-tenth as much in remittances as it did during the period of prosperity.

This precipitous decline in income plunged the region into misery. Kabyle peasants could not afford to buy high-priced wheat with what they were able to earn by selling their own produce at low prices. They had previously purchased the food they needed, saving themselves from starvation by relying on the labor of their émigré sons. When that source of income was taken away, they found themselves defenseless against hunger. What I saw was the result, and I want to describe the situation as economically as possible so that readers may experience for themselves its distress and absurdity.

According to an official report, 40 percent of Kabyle families are living today on less than 1,000 francs per year, which is to say, less than 100 francs per month. Think about what that means. According to the same report, only 5 percent of families have more than 500 francs per month. Given that the typical family in the region consists of five or six people, you begin to have some idea of the indescribable penury of the Kabyle peasantry. I believe I can state that at least 50 percent of the population lives on herbs and roots in between government handouts of grain.

In Bordj-Menaïel, for example, of the 27,000 Kabyles in the commune, 10,000 live in poverty, and only 1,000 eat a normal diet. At the grain distribution that took place on the day I arrived, I saw nearly 500 impoverished peasants patiently awaiting their turn to receive a few liters of wheat. On that same day I was shown the local miracle: an old woman, bent double, who weighed only 25 kilograms. Each indigent was given roughly 10 kilos of wheat. In Bordj-Menaïel, handouts occur at monthly intervals, but in other places they take place only once every three months. Now, a family of eight needs approximately 120 kilos of wheat for just one month's worth of bread. I was told that the indigents I saw had to make their 10 kilos last the entire month, supplementing their meager grain supply with roots and the stems of thistle, which the Kabyles, with bitter irony, call the "artichoke of the ass."

In the Tizi-Ouzou district, some women walk as much as 30 or 40 kilometers to receive similar handouts. Without the charity of a local pastor, these poor women would have had no place to spend the night.

There are other signs of desperate poverty as well. In the Tizi-Ouzou "tribe," for example, wheat has become a luxury good. The best families eat a mix of wheat and sorghum. Poor families have been known to pay as much as 20 francs a quintal for wild acorns. The usual menu of a poor family in this tribe consists of a barley-cake and a soup of thistle stems and mallow roots with a small amount of olive oil. But last year's olive harvest was small, so this year there is no oil. The diet is similar throughout Kabylia; not a single village is an exception to the rule.

Early one morning in Tizi-Ouzou, I saw children in rags fighting with dogs over some garbage. To my questions a Kabyle responded: "It's like that every morning." Another resident of the village explained that during the winter, the ill-fed and ill-housed people had come up with a way to keep warm and get some sleep. They formed a circle around a wood fire, moving about occasionally to avoid getting stiff. So the circle of bodies was in constant motion, creeping along the ground. But this expedient probably isn't enough to keep everyone alive, because the forest regulations prohibit these poor people from picking up twigs where they find them, and it is not uncommon for the authorities to punish offenders by seizing their only worldly possession, the crusty, emaciated ass they use to carry home their bundles of twigs. In the Tizi-Ouzou area, moreover, things have gotten so bad that private charity had to step in. Every Wednesday, the subprefect pays *out of his own pocket* so that 50 young Kabyles can enjoy a meal of bouillon and bread. With that they can hold out until the next monthly grain distribution. The Soeurs Blanches (Sisters of Our

Lady of North Africa) and Pastor Rolland also help out with these charitable dinners.

———

Some readers may be thinking, "But these are special cases. . . . It's the Depression, etc. And in any event the figures are *meaningless*." I confess that I cannot understand this way of looking at the matter. I concede that statistics are meaningless, but if I say that the resident of Azouza whom I went to see belonged to a family of 10 children of whom only 2 survived, I am not giving you statistics or abstract arguments but a stark and revealing fact. Nor do I need to mention the number of students in the schools around Fort-National who fainted from hunger. It's enough to know that they did and that it will happen again if these poor wretches do not get help. It is enough to know that teachers in the school at Talam-Aïach saw their students come to class this past October completely naked and covered with lice, and that they gave them clothes and shaved their heads. It is enough to know that among the students who leave school at 11 A.M. because their village is so far away from the schoolhouse, only 1 out of 60 eats barleycakes, while the others lunch on an onion or a couple of figs.

When grain was distributed in Fort-National, I questioned a child who was carrying a small sack of barley on his back.

"How many days is that supposed to last?"

"Two weeks."

"How many people in your family?"

"Five."

"Is that all you have to eat?"

"Yes."

"You have no figs?"

"No."

"Do you have olive oil to put on your flatcakes?"

"No, we use water."

And with a suspicious look he proceeded on his way.

Is that not enough? When I look at my notes, I see twice as many equally revolting realities, and I despair of ever being able to convey them all. It must be done, however, and the whole truth must be told.

————

For now, I must end this survey of the suffering and hunger of an entire people. The reader will have seen, at least, that misery here is not just a word or a theme for meditation. It exists. It cries out in desperation. What have we done about it, and do we have the right to avert our eyes? I am not sure that anyone will understand. But I do know that after returning from a visit to the "tribe" of Tizi-Ouzou, I climbed with a Kabyle friend to the heights overlooking the town. From there we watched the night fall. And at that hour, when the shadows descending from the mountains across this splendid land can soften even the hardest of hearts, I knew that there was no peace for those who, on the other side of the valley, were gathering around a spoiled barleycake. I also knew that while it would have been comforting to surrender to the startling grandeur of that night, the misery gathered around the glowing fires across the way placed the beauty of this world under a kind of ban.

"Let's go down now, shall we?" my friend said.

2

Destitution (continued)

One evening, while walking in the streets of Tizi-Ouzou after traveling around the region, I asked one of my companions if it "was like this everywhere." His answer was that I would soon see worse. We then walked for quite some time around the native village, where faint light from the shops mingled with music, folk dancing, and indistinct chatter in the dark streets.

And in fact I did see worse.

I knew that thistle stems were a staple of the Kabyle diet, and I discovered that this was indeed the case everywhere. What I did not know, however, was that last year, five Kabyle children from the Abbo region died after eating poisonous roots. I knew that not enough grain was being distributed to keep the Kabyles alive. But I did not know that the distributions were actually causing them to die, or that last winter, four elderly women who had gone to Michelet to collect grain handouts froze to death in the snow on their way home to their remote *douar* (village).

Yet everything is as it was meant to be. In Adni, only 40 of 106 schoolchildren eat enough to stave off hunger. Nearly everyone in the village is unemployed, and grain distributions are rare. In the douars of the commune of Michelet, the number of unemployed per douar is estimated to be nearly 500. And in the poorest places, such as Akbils, Aït-Yahia, and Abi-Youcef, the unemployment rate is even higher. In the entire commune there are some 4,000 able-bodied workers without jobs. Thirty-five of the 110 students at the school in Azerou-Kollal eat only one meal a day. Four-fifths of the people in Maillot are said to be destitute, and grain is distributed there only once every three months. In Ouadhias, there are 300 indigents in a population of 7,500, but in the Sidi-Aïch region, 60 percent of the people are indigent. In the village of El-Flay, above the center of Sidi-Aïch, some families go two or three days without eating. Most of the families in this village supplement their daily diet with roots and cakes of pine seed picked up from the forest floor. But when they dare to gather pinecones, they often run afoul of the law, because the rangers mercilessly enforce the regulations.

If this litany of horrors is not convincing, I will add that 2,000 of the 2,500 Kabyle residents of the El-Kseur commune are paupers. For their entire day's ration, agricultural workers carry with them a quarter of a barleycake and a small flask of olive oil. Families supplement their roots and herbs with nettles. If cooked for hours, this plant can complement the usual pauper's meal. The same is true in the douars around Azazga. The native villages in the vicinity of Dellys also number among the poorest in the region. In Beni-Sliem for instance, an incredible 96 percent of the population is indigent. The harsh land there yields nothing. Residents are reduced to gathering fallen wood to burn for charcoal, which they then try to sell in Dellys. I say "try to sell" because they do not have vendor licenses, so that half the time their charcoal is seized along with the ass used to transport it. Villagers have therefore taken to sneaking into Dellys by night, but the rangers remain vigilant around the clock. When animals are seized, they are sent to the pound. The charcoal burner must then pay the pound fee in addition to a fine in order to retrieve his ass.

If he cannot pay, he is arrested and sent to prison, where at least he can eat. So it is in that sense and that sense only that one can say without irony that the sale of charcoal feeds the people of Beni-Sliem.

What could I possibly add to facts such as these? Mark them well. Imagine the lives of hopelessness and desperation that lie behind them. If you find this normal, then say so. But if you find it repellent, take action. And if you find it unbelievable, then please, go and see for yourself.

———

What remedies have been proposed to alleviate such distress? Only one: charity. Grain is distributed, and with this grain and cash assistance so-called "charity workshops" have been created.

About the distributions of grain I will be brief. Experience has shown how absurd they are. A handout of 12 liters of grain every two or three months to families with four or five children is the equivalent of spitting in the ocean. Millions are spent every year, and those millions do no good. I do not think that charitable feelings are useless. But I do think that in some cases the results of charity are useless and that a constructive social policy would therefore be preferable.

Note, too, that the selection of beneficiaries of these handouts is usually left to the discretion of the local *caïd* (village chieftain) or municipal councilors, who are not necessarily impartial. Some say that the most recent general council elections in Tizi-Ouzou were bought with grain from the distributions. It is not my business to investigate whether or not this is true, but the mere fact that it is being said is itself a condemnation of the method of selection. In any case, I know for a fact that in Issers, grain was denied to indigents who voted for the Algerian People's Party. What is more, nearly everyone in Kabylia complains about the poor quality of the grain that is distributed. Some of it no doubt comes from our national surplus, but part of it is outdated grain disposed of by army warehouses. So that in Michelet, for example, the barley that was given out was so bitter that even the animals wouldn't eat it, and some Kabyles told me with straight faces that they envied the horses of the gendarmerie, because they at least ate food that was inspected by a veterinarian.

―――――――

To deal with unemployment, many communes have organized charity workshops, where indigents do useful work for which they are paid 8 to 10 francs a day, half in grain, half in cash. The communes of Fort-National, Michelet, Maillot, and Port-Gueydon, among others, have organized such workshops, which offer the advantage of preserving the dignity of the men receiving assistance. But they also have one important drawback: in communes where all the grain available for assistance goes to the workshops, invalids who are unable to work receive no aid. Furthermore, since the number of workshop jobs is limited, workers must be rotated, with priority for those who are able to work two days straight. In Tizi-Ouzou, workers are employed for 4 days out of every 40, for which they receive 20 liters of grain. Once again, the millions that are spent amount to spitting in the ocean.

Finally, I must say something about a practice that has become widespread but which should be the object of vigorous protest. In all communes except for Port-Gueydon, back taxes owed by indigents (because indigents are subject to taxation even though they cannot pay) are subtracted from the cash component of their wages. There are no words harsh enough to condemn such cruelty. If the charity workshops are meant to help people who are dying of hunger, there is a reason for their existence—an honorable reason, even if the results are risible. But if their effect is to make people work in order to die of hunger, whereas previously they died of hunger without working, then the workshops are nothing more than a despicable device for exploiting misery.

———

I do not want to end this portrait of penury without pointing out that it does not give the full measure of Kabylia's distress. To add insult to injury, winter follows summer every year. Right now, nature is treating these poor people relatively kindly. No one is cold. The donkey paths are still passable. Wild thistle can still be harvested for another two months. Roots are abundant. People can eat raw greens. What looks to us like extreme poverty is a blessed time for the Kabyle peasant. But once snow falls and blocks the roads and cold gnaws at malnourished bodies and makes rudimentary huts uninhabitable, a long winter of unspeakable suffering begins.

So before moving on to other aspects of wretched Kabylia's existence, I would like to dispose of certain arguments often heard in Algeria, arguments that use the supposed Kabyle "mentality" to excuse the current situation. These arguments are beneath contempt. It is despicable, for example, to say that these people can adapt to anything. Mr. Albert Lebrun[1] himself, if he had to live on 200 francs a month, would adapt to living under bridges and surviving on garbage and crusts of bread. When it comes to clinging to life, there is something in man capable of overcoming the most abject miseries. It is despicable to say that these people don't have the same needs we do. If they don't, then it is high time we

1. The president of France from 1932 to 1940.—*Trans.*

showed them what they are missing. It is curious to note how the alleged qualities of a people are used to justify the debased condition in which they are kept, and how the proverbial sobriety of the Kabyle peasant lends legitimacy to his hunger. This is not the right way to look at things, and it is not the way we will look at things, because preconceived ideas and prejudices become odious when applied to a world in which people are freezing to death and children are reduced to foraging like animals even though they lack the instincts that would prevent them from eating things that will kill them. The truth is that we are living every day alongside people whose condition is that of the European peasantry of three centuries ago, and yet we, and we alone, are unmoved by their desperate plight.

3

Wages

People who are dying of hunger generally have only one way to survive: by working. I beg your pardon for stating such an obvious fact. But the present situation in Kabylia proves that knowledge of this fact is not as universal as it might seem. I said previously that half the Kabyle population is unemployed and three-quarters of the people are undernourished. This discrepancy is not the result of mistaken arithmetic. It simply proves that those who are not out of work still do not have enough to eat.

I had been alerted to the fact that wages in Kabylia were insufficient; I did not know that they were insulting. I had been told that the working day exceeded the legal limit. I did not know that it was close to twice that long. I do not wish to be shrill, but I am obliged to say that the labor regime in Kabylia is one of slave labor, for I see no other word to describe a system in which workers toil for 10 to 12 hours per day for an average wage of 6 to 10 francs.

I will enumerate wage levels by region without further commentary. First, however, I want to say that although these figures might seem extraordinary, I can vouch for them. I am looking right now at the time cards of farmworkers on the Sabaté-Tracol estates in the region of Bordj-Menaïel. They bear the date of the current two-week pay period, the name of the worker, a serial number, and the nominal wage. On one card I see the figure 8 francs, on another 7, and on a third 6. In the time column, I see that the worker who earned 6 francs worked four days in the two-week period. Can the reader imagine what this means?

Even if the worker in question worked 25 days per month, he would earn only 150 francs, with which he would have to feed a family of several children for 30 days. Can anyone read this without feeling outrage? How many of you reading this article would be able to live on such a sum?

––––––

Before continuing with my narrative, let me state some facts. The wages I just mentioned are from the region of Bordj-Menaïel. I should add that the sirens at Tracol Farms sound during the high season (which is now) at 4 A.M., 11 A.M., 12 noon, and 7 P.M. That adds up to 14 hours of work. The communal workers in the village are paid 9 francs a day. After a protest by native municipal councilors, wages were increased to 10 francs. At Tabacoop, in the same region, the daily wage is 9 francs. In Tizi-Ouzou, the average wage is 7 francs for 12 hours of work. Employees of the commune get 12 francs.

Kabyle farmers in the region employ women to do weeding. For the same 12 hours of work, *they are paid 3.5 francs.* In Fort-National, Kabyle farmers are no more generous than their European counterparts, paying workers 6 to 7 francs a day. Women are paid 4 francs and given a flatcake as well. Communal employees receive 9 to 11 francs.

In the region of Djemaa-Saridj, where the soil is richer, men are paid 8 to 10 francs for 10 hours of work, and women get 5 francs. Around Michelet, the average farm wage is 5 francs plus food for 10 hours of work. The communal wage is 11 to 12 francs, but back taxes are withheld from the worker's pay without notice. The amount withheld is sometimes equal to the *total wage*. The average withholding is 20 francs per week.

In Ouadhias, the farm wage is 6 to 8 francs. Women get 3 to 5 francs for picking olives, while communal workers receive 10 to 11 francs less withholding for back taxes.

In the Maillot region, workers get 9 to 10 francs for an unlimited number of hours per day. For olive picking, the compensation has been set at 8 francs per quintal of olives harvested. A family of four can harvest an average of 2 quintals per day. The family therefore receives 4 francs per person.

In the Sidi-Aïch region, the wage is 6 francs plus a flatcake and figs. One local agricultural firm pays its workers 7 francs without food. Workers are also hired by the year for 1,000 francs plus food.

In the plain of El-Kseur, a colonized region, male workers are paid 10 francs, females 5 francs, and children who are employed to trim vines are paid 3 francs. Finally, in the region that stretches from Dellys to Port-Gueydon, the average wage is 6 to 10 francs for 12 hours of work.

I will end this depressing list with two remarks. First, the workers have never rebelled against this mistreatment. Only in 1936, at Beni-Yenni, did workers involved in building a road, for which they were paid *5 francs per day,* go on strike, winning a raise to 10 francs a day. Those workers were not unionized.

Second, I want to mention that the unjustifiable length of the working day is aggravated by the fact that the typical Kabyle worker lives a long way from where he works. Some must travel more than 10 kilometers round trip. After returning home at 10 at night, they must set out again for work at 3 in the morning after only a few hours of heavy sleep. You may be wondering why they bother to go home at all. My answer is simply that they cling to the inconceivable ambition of spending a few quiet moments in a home that is their only joy in life as well as the object of all their concerns.

———————

There are reasons for this state of affairs. The official estimate of the value of a day's labor service is 17 francs. If employers can pay a daily wage of only 6 francs, the reason is that widespread unemployment has put workers in competition with one another. Both settlers and Kabyle landowners are so aware of this that some administrators have been reluctant to increase communal wages in order to avoid angering these employers.

In Beni-Yenni, owing to circumstances about which I will say more in a moment, a program of public works was inaugurated. Unemployment decreased sharply, and *workers were paid 22 francs a day*. This proves that exploitation alone is the cause of low wages. None of the other reasons sometimes advanced to explain the status quo makes sense.

Settlers allege that Kabyle workers often change jobs and that they therefore pay them "temporary" wages. But in Kabylia today, all wages are temporary, and this wretched excuse merely covers unpardonable self-interest.

Before concluding, I must say a word about the widespread idea that native labor is inferior to European labor. It is of course a product of the general contempt that settlers feel for the unfortunate natives of this country. As I see it, this contempt discredits those who profess it. I say that it is wrong to say that the productivity of Kabyle workers is inadequate, because if it were, the foremen who keep close watch on them would take it upon themselves to improve it.

Of course it is true that at some work sites one sees workers who are unsteady on their feet and incapable of lifting a shovel, but that is because they have not eaten. It is a perverse logic that says that a man is weak because he hasn't enough to eat and that therefore one should pay him less because he is weak.

There is no way out of this situation. Kabylia cannot be saved from starvation by distributing grain. It can only be saved by reducing unemployment and monitoring wages. These things can and should be done immediately.

I learned today that the colonial authorities, anxious to demonstrate concern for the native population, will reward veterans with medals signifying their military service. May I add that I write these lines not with irony but with a certain sadness? I see nothing wrong with rewarding courage and loyalty. But many of the people who are dying of hunger in Kabylia today also served. I wonder how they will present the bit of metal signifying their loyalty to France to their starving children.

4

Education

The Kabyles' thirst for learning and taste for study have become legendary. In addition to their natural predisposition to learning and practical intelligence, they quickly grasped the fact that education could be an instrument of emancipation. It is not unusual these days for a village to offer to provide a room or funding or free labor for the purpose of creating a school. Nor is it unusual to see these offers remain without response from the authorities. And Kabyles are not just worried about educating boys. I have not visited a single major town in Kabylia without hearing how eager people are for girls' schools as well. And there is not a single existing school anywhere in Kabylia that is not obliged to turn students away.

Indeed, a shortage of schools is *the* educational issue in Kabylia today. The region lacks schools, but it does not lack money for education. I will explain this paradox in a moment. Leaving aside the dozen large schools that have been built in recent years, most Kabyle schools date from the late nineteenth century, when the Algerian budget was decided in metropolitan France.

From 1892 to 1912, no schools were built in the region. At the time, the Joly-Jean-Marie Plan envisioned the construction of numerous schools at 5,000 francs apiece. On February 7, 1914, Governor General Lutaud formally announced that 22 new schools and 62 classrooms would be built in Algeria every year. Had these goals been even half realized, the 900,000 native children who are today without schools would have received an education.

For reasons that I need not go into here, the official plan was scrapped. I will summarize the results of this decision in one figure: today, only one-tenth of school-age Kabyle children actually attend school.

Does this mean that Algerian authorities neglected education entirely? The issue is complex. In a recent speech, M. Le Beau [the governor general] stated that several million francs had been devoted to native education, but the statistics I am about to give prove unequivocally that this spending has done little to improve matters. Hence, to put it bluntly, these millions were badly spent, as I propose to show in what follows. But let me describe the situation first.

———

As one might expect, the country's economic and tourist centers are well served. What interests me here, however, is the fate of the douars and people of Kabylia. I might begin by observing that Tizi-Ouzou, which does have a fine native school with room for 600 students, turns away 500 prospective additional students every year.

In one school I visited in Oumalous, the teachers were forced this past October to turn away a dozen applicants for each class. And there were already 60–80 more students per class than the school was really equipped to handle.

In Beni-Douala, one class serves 86 pupils, some of whom must sit on the floor between benches or on the platform at the front of the room, while others are forced to stand. In Djemaa-Saridj, a splendid school with 250 students had to reject 50 additional applicants in October. The school in Adni, with 106 students, turned away another dozen after dismissing all students above the age of 13.

The situation in the vicinity Michelet is even more revealing. The Aguedal douar, with a population of 11,000, has only one school with two classrooms. The Ittomagh douar, with a population of 10,000 Kabyles, has no school at all. In Beni-Ouacif, the Bou-Abderrahmane school has just turned away more than 100 students.

The village of Aït-Aïlem has maintained a classroom for the past two years, but no teacher has yet been assigned to it.

In the Sidi-Aïch region, 200 prospective students turned up at the beginning of the term in the village of Vieux-Marché. Only 15 were accepted.

The douar of Ikedjane, with a population of 15,000, lacks even a single classroom. The douar of Timzrit, with a similar population, has a one-room schoolhouse. Iyadjadjène (pop. 5,000) has no school. Azrou-N'Bechar (pop. 6,000) has no school.

It has been estimated that 80 percent of the children in the region are deprived of education. I would translate this statistic by saying that nearly 10,000 Kabyle children are left to play every day in the mud of the gutters.

As for the commune of Maillot, I am looking at a list of schools per douar and per capita. Even though this essay is not intended for the society pages, I am afraid that it would be tedious to recount this information in detail. I will mention only that there are just nine classrooms in the region for 30,000 Kabyles. In the Dellys region, in the douar of Beni-Sliem, whose extreme poverty I described previously, there is not a single classroom for a population of 9,000.

The laudable decision of the colonial authorities to educate girls was taken only recently, and 9 out of 10 douars are surely not providing female education. It would be ungracious to try to assign responsibility for this failure. What needs to be said, however, is that Kabyles consider the education of girls to be extremely important and unanimously favor its expansion.

Indeed, it is quite moving to see how clearly some Kabyle males recognize the gap that the unilateral education of boys has created between themselves and their women. As one of them told me, "'Home' is now nothing more than a word, a social convention without living content. We are painfully aware that it is impossible to share our feelings with our wives. Give us girls' schools or this fracture will upset the equilibrium of life here."

———

Does this mean that nothing has been done to educate the Kabyles? Not at all. Some splendid schools have been built—nearly a dozen in all, I believe. Each of these schools cost between 700,000 and one million francs. The most sumptuous are surely the schools in Djemaa-Saridj, Tizi-Rached, Tizi-Ouzou, and Tililit. But these schools regularly turn away prospective students, and they do not meet any of the region's needs.

What Kabylia needs is not a few palatial establishments. It needs many sound and modest schools. I believe that all teachers will back me up when I say that they can live without tiled walls, and all they need is a clean, comfortable classroom. And I also believe that they love their work well enough, as they prove every day in their lonely and difficult teaching in rural areas, that they would rather have two classrooms than a useless pergola.

I saw a symbol of this absurd educational policy on the Port-Gueydon road in the region of Aghrib, one of the harshest in Kabylia. From a hilltop one glimpsed a patch of ocean nestled in a recess between mountain ranges, but that was the only beauty to be seen. As far as the eye could see, arid, rocky land covered with bright broom and lentisk stretched into the distance beneath the merciless sun. And there, in the midst of this vast wasteland devoid of any visible sign of humanity, stood the sumptuous Aghrib school, a veritable symbol of futility.

Here I feel obliged to explain my thought at some length. I don't know what one ought to think about what one Kabyle man said to me: "Don't you see, the goal was to give us the smallest number of classrooms with the maximum expenditure of capital." In any case, my impression is that these schools were built for tourists and investigating commissions and that they sacrifice the basic needs of the native people on the altar of prestige.

Such a policy strikes me as particularly unfortunate. If there is any justification for prestige, it must come not from impressive appearances but from profound generosity and fraternal understanding.

In the meantime, the same appropriation that built these palatial schools could have been used to build three extra classrooms to serve the students who must be turned away every fall. I have looked into the cost of building a typical two-room schoolhouse of modern and comfortable design along with a couple of adjoining rooms for teachers' housing. Such a school can be built for 200,000 francs. With what it takes to build one palatial school, one can build three of these old-fashioned schoolhouses. This, I think, is enough to judge a policy that is tantamount to giving a 1,000-franc doll to a child who has not eaten for three days.

———

The Kabyles want schools, then, as they want bread. But I am also convinced that a more general educational reform is needed. When I put the question to Kabyles, they were unanimous in their answers. They will have more schools on the day that the artificial barrier between European and indigenous schools is removed—on the day when two peoples destined to understand each other begin to make each other's acquaintance on the benches of a shared schoolhouse.

Of course, I am under no illusions as to the powers of education. But those who speak so easily about the uselessness of teaching have nevertheless benefited from it themselves. If the authorities really want assimilation, and if these worthy Kabyles are indeed French, then it makes no sense to start off by separating them from the French. If I understand them correctly, this is all they are asking for. And my own feeling is that mutual comprehension will begin only when there is joint schooling. I say "begin" because it must be said that to date there is no mutual understanding, which is why our political authorities have made so many mistakes. All that is needed, however, is a genuinely extended hand—as I have recently discovered for myself. But it is up to us to break down the walls that keep us apart.

The Political Future

Without pretending to be a distinguished economist, I would like to consider in purely commonsensical terms what political, economic, and social future one might like to see for Kabylia. I have said enough about the misery of this region, but one cannot simply describe such distress without saying something about what response is called for.

I would also like to say something about method. In the face of such an urgent situation, we must act quickly, and it would be foolish to contemplate a utopian scheme or advocate impossible solutions. That is why each of the suggestions below starts not with risky principles but with experiments that have already been tried or are currently under way in the region. And of course nothing in this story is invented; everything is taken from reality. As a talented speaker recently put it, in politics there are no copyrights. My goal is to help a friendly people, and the only purpose of these proposals is to serve that goal.

One must start from the principle that if anyone can improve the lot of the Kabyles, change has to begin with the Kabyles themselves. Three-quarters of the population lives under the mixed

regime, village-chieftain system.[1] Many other writers have criti-
cized this political form, which bears only a distant resemblance to
democracy, and I will not repeat their criticisms here. The abuses
due to this system have been abundantly documented. But even
within the framework of the mixed commune, the Kabyles now
have an opportunity to demonstrate their administrative skills.

With the law of April 27, 1937, a generous legislature opened
the possibility of transforming certain Algerian douars into communes run by the native population under the supervision of a
French administrator. Several experiments of this sort have been
carried out in Arab and Kabyle regions. If these attempts are
deemed successful, then there is no reason to delay extending the
douar-commune system. As it happens, an interesting experiment
is under way right now in Kabylia, and I wanted to see it for myself. Since January 1938, the douar of Oumalous, a few kilometers
from Fort-National, has been operating as a douar-commune under the leadership of M. Hadjeres. Thanks to his kindness and
intelligent competence, I was able to observe the operation of this
douar in person and document its achievements. The Oumalous
douar includes 18 villages and a population of 1,200. A town hall
was built in the geographical center, along with several additional
buildings. This town hall is like any other town hall, but for residents of the douar it has the advantage of allowing them to complete administrative formalities without extensive travel. In May
1938, the town hall issued no fewer than 517 administrative docu-

1. For administrative purposes, the Algerian colony was divided into *départements*. Each
département was further divided into "mixed communes." At the same time there were
also entities known as *communes de plein exercice,* here translated as "full-fledged communes." There were also "douar-communes," created by a senatus consult of May 23,
1863, governed by an assembly known as the *djemaa,* headed by a native chieftain known
as the *caïd.* In this essay Camus discusses a reform under which mixed and douar-
communes were transformed into full-fledged communes.—*Trans.*

ments to citizens of the commune, and in the same year it facilitated the emigration of 515 Kabyles.

With a minimal budget of 200,000 francs, this miniature municipality, staffed by Kabyle officials elected by Kabyle voters, has presided for the past year and a half over an indigenous community in which complaints are rare. For the first time, Kabyles are dealing with officials whose work they can monitor and whom they can approach to talk things over rather than merely obey in silence.

The Kabyles quite rightly attach considerable value to these changes. One therefore cannot be too careful in criticizing recent experiments. M. Hadjeres has nevertheless proposed certain improvements, which strike me as reasonable. To date, voters have been obliged to vote for slates of candidates, with the winning slate then electing its own president. The douar retains its traditional caïd, however, and remains under the supervision of a colonial administrator. The respective functions of these three officials—president of the commune, caïd, and administrator—are not clearly defined, and it would be useful to clarify and delineate them.

Furthermore, the experiments with the douar-commune system have provoked a number of protests, whose motives I will not discuss, and elicited a number of criticisms that call for further examination. A recent series of articles argued that the douar was an artificial administrative unit and that the creation of douar-communes risked bringing together villages and factions with opposing interests. In most cases this is simply not true, although it does sometimes happen. In any case, the same series of articles proposed establishing native rule at the level of the village rather than the douar, and this is a very bad idea. For one thing, most villages have little if any resources. There are villages, for instance, whose only common property is a single ash or fig tree. For another, there are far too many Kabyle villages to allow an adequate level of administrative supervision.

To be sure, it would be a good idea to group villages that share a common geographical and cultural situation. Perpetuating old divisions in a mixed communal framework would result in administrative complications that are best avoided.

———

It therefore seems preferable to amend the existing legislation without changing the basic administrative framework. On this point, I can do no better than to summarize the plan that M. Hadjeres explained to me with remarkable lucidity. Essentially, his plan comes down to extending democracy at the douar-commune level and introducing a kind of proportional representation. If the goal is to avoid conflicts of interest, M. Hadjeres is of the opinion that the best way to do this is to allow all interests to be expressed. He therefore proposes that voters no longer be asked to vote for a slate of candidates. Instead, each village should elect its own representatives. These representatives would then come together to form a municipal council, which would elect its own president. In this way, competition among villages within a douar would be eliminated. In addition, village elections would be based on proportional representation, with each village entitled to one representative for every 800 citizens. In this way, intra-village rivalries would also be eliminated. As a result, the *djemaa* of Oumalous would be reduced from 20 members to 16. Finally, M. Hadjeres envisions the transformation into communes of all the douars of the mixed commune of Fort-National, along with the creation of a single budget combining all available resources, which would then be shared among douars in proportion to their needs and population. This would establish a small federative republic in the heart of Kabyle territory, a republic inspired by deeply democratic principles. As I listened to the president of Oumalous, I appreciated his remarkable lucidity and common sense, which might well serve as an example for many of our democratic officials. In any case, I have set forth his proposal as he described it. I hope that the administration will know how to put it to good use.

———

If the Oumalous experiment is deemed to have been a success, there is no reason not to extend it elsewhere. Many douars are waiting to be transformed into communes. Around Michelet, for example, there are some that seem even more likely to succeed than Oumalous. They have markets that handle a substantial volume of trade. If the administration wants this experiment to succeed, then these douars, such as Menguellet and Ouacif, should become communes. Frequently, however, the mixed commune opposes this change for douars with markets on the grounds that these markets provide revenue to the commune (as much as 150,000 francs per year in some cases). But these douars are virtually the only viable ones. If, moreover, one believes that the douar-commune should within a short period of time replace the mixed commune altogether, then one will agree that it is the latter that should be sacrificed.

Furthermore, the authorities should not hesitate to transform other douars, such as Ouadhias, into full-fledged communes. There are already more than 100 French voters in the center of Ouadhias. Its market brings in 70,000 francs a year, and it yields 100,000 francs in taxes. This would be a good place to experiment with allowing French citizens of Kabyle descent to gain experience in public affairs.

———————

In any case, such a generous policy would clear the way for the administrative emancipation of Kabylia. To achieve that goal, it is enough today to really want it. It can be pursued in parallel with material assistance to this unfortunate region. We have made enough mistakes along the way to be able to benefit from the lessons that failure always has to teach. For instance, I know of few arguments more specious than that of personal status[2] when it comes to extending political rights to natives, but when applied to Kabylia, the argument becomes ridiculous, because it was we French who imposed a personal status on the Kabyles by Arabizing their country with the caïd system and introducing the Arabic language. It ill behooves us today to reproach the Kabyles for embracing the status we imposed on them.

That the Kabyle people are ready for greater independence and self-rule was obvious to me one morning when, after returning from Oumalous, I fell into conversation with M. Hadjeres. We had gone to a gap in the mountains through which one could see the vast extent of a douar that stretched all the way to the horizon. My companion named the various villages for me and explained what life was like in each one. He described how the village imposed solidarity on each of its members, forcing all residents to attend every funeral in order to make sure that the poor man's burial was no less impressive than the rich man's. He also told me

2. The law of personal status is a province of French law dealing with individual and family matters. In some colonies, the personal status of natives allowed for them to be treated differently from French nationals without violating the principle of equality before the law.—*Trans.*

that banishment from the community was the worst possible punishment, which no one could bear. As we looked down on that
vast, sunbaked land from a dizzying height, the trees resembled
clouds of vapor steaming up from the hot soil, and I understood
what bound these people to one another and made them cling to
their land. I also understood how little they needed in order to live
in harmony with themselves. So how could I fail to understand
their desire to take charge of their own lives and their hunger to
become at last what they truly are: courageous, conscientious human beings from whom we could humbly take lessons in dignity
and justice?

The Economic and Social Future

Kabylia has too many people and not enough grain. It consumes more than it produces. Its labor, compensated with ridiculously low wages, is not sufficient to pay for what it consumes. Its émigrés, whose numbers dwindle year after year, can no longer make up for this trade deficit.

If we want to return Kabylia to prosperity, save its people from famine, and do our duty toward the Kabyle people, we must therefore change everything about the region's economy.

Common sense suggests that if Kabylia consumes more than it produces, we must first try to increase the purchasing power of the Kabyle people so that the wages of their labor can compensate for the shortages of their production. We must also try to reduce the gap between imports and exports by increasing the latter as much as possible.

These are the main lines of a policy that everyone agrees is essential. The two aspects of this policy must not be separated, however. There is no way to raise the standard of living in Kabylia without paying people more and paying more for their products. It is not just humanity that is trampled underfoot when people are paid six francs a day for their work, it is also logic. And the low prices paid for Kabylia's cash crops are an affront not only to justice but also to common sense.

In this essay I will review a number of the constant themes of this inquiry. Kabyle labor is paid as it is only because of unemployment and the latitude allowed to employers. Wages will therefore not become normal until unemployment has been reduced, competition in the labor market has been eliminated, and tariffs have been restored.

Until labor inspectors are actually dispatched to Kabylia, it is desirable that the state employ as many workers as possible. Monitoring of the market will then be automatic. Unemployment must be reduced in three stages: first by a program of public works, second by the establishment of job training programs, and third by the organization of emigration.

Public works programs are of course part of every demagogic political platform. But the essence of demagogy is that programs are proposed but never implemented. Here, the goal is the opposite.

To undertake public works in a country that has no need of them is indeed a waste of public funds. But need I point out how sorely Kabylia lacks for roads and water? Not only would a major public works program eliminate the bulk of unemployment and raise wages to a normal level; it would also yield surplus economic value for Kabylia, and sooner or later we will reap the benefits.

This policy has already been initiated. Where it was systematically pursued in the commune of Port-Gueydon and the douar of Beni-Yenni, the results were immediately apparent. Port-Gueydon now boasts of 17 new fountains and a number of new roads. Beni-Yenni is one of the wealthiest douars in Kabylia, and its workers are paid 22 francs a day.

The major criticism that one can make, however, is that these experiments remain isolated. And large amounts of public funds have been dispersed in small subsidies that have had virtually no effect. Government officials regularly ask, "Where are we to find the money?" But for now, at least, the problem is not to come up with new funding but just to use money that has already been appropriated.

Nearly 600 million francs have been directed toward Kabylia. It is now 10 days since I tried to describe the horrifying results. What is needed now is an intelligent and comprehensive plan that can be systematically implemented. We want nothing to do with politics as usual, with half measures and compromises, small handouts and scattered subsidies. Kabylia wants the opposite of business as usual: namely, smart and generous policy. It will take vision to pull together all the appropriated sums, scattered subsidies, and wasted charity if Kabylia is to be saved by the Kabyles themselves, if the dignity of these peasants is to be restored through useful labor paid at a just wage.

We managed to come up with the money to give the countries of Europe nearly 400 billion francs, all of which is now gone forever. It seems unlikely that we cannot come up with one-hundredth that amount to improve the lot of people whom we have not yet made French, to be sure, but from whom we demand the sacrifices of French citizens.

Furthermore, wages are so low only because the Kabyles do not qualify for protection under existing labor laws. That is where job training for both industrial and agricultural workers comes in. There are occupational training schools in Kabylia. In Michelet, there is a school for blacksmiths, carpenters, and masons. It has trained good workers, some of whom live in Michelet itself. But the school can train only a dozen students at a time, and that is not enough.

There are also schools in arboriculture, like the one in Mechtras, but it graduates only 30 students every two years. This is an experiment, not an institution.

These efforts must now be expanded, and every center must be equipped with a vocational training school to train people whose skills and desire to assimilate are proverbial.

All of Kabylia's problems are related, moreover. There is no better illustration of this than the fact that there is no point training skilled workers if they cannot find jobs. For now, however, all the jobs are in metropolitan France. So no training policy will work unless something is done to help Kabyles emigrate.

To that end, the first thing to do is to simplify the formalities, and the second is to assist with emigration. Right now it is possible to help Kabyles find jobs in farming. I am not speaking of the offers coming from the Niger Office. There is no point sending Kabyle peasants to die for the benefit of private firms in a lethal foreign environment. But the colonial authorities could still distribute nearly 200,000 hectares of land in Algeria if they chose to.

In Kabylia itself, near Boghni, an experiment of this type is under way in the Bou-Mani estates. Meanwhile, people are fleeing the south of France, and we had to bring in tens of thousands of Italians to colonize our own soil.

Today, those Italians are returning home. There is no reason why Kabyles cannot colonize this region. We are told that "Kabyles are too attached to their mountains to leave them." My answer is first of all that there are presently 50,000 Kabyles in France who have already left those same mountains. In addition, I will mention the response of one Kabyle peasant to whom I put the question: "You are forgetting that we do not have anything to eat. We have no choice."

I anticipate the next objection: "But these Kabyles will eventually abandon their land and return home." This may well be true, but is there anyone who does not see that Kabyles have been coming to France generation after generation and that no landowner will leave his land until he has sold it to someone younger than himself?

In any case, these few measures should suffice to raise the wages of Kabyle workers to a decent level. And it bears repeating that the sums already appropriated should suffice to get the project under way. The policy will begin to yield benefits when its extension becomes inevitable. But the fruits of such a policy cannot truly be reaped unless the prices paid for Kabylia's agricultural production are also raised at the same time.

————

Once again, common sense points the way toward a constructive policy. Although the region does produce a small amount of grain, its main cash crops are figs and olives. Since it is futile to try to counter the forces of nature, attention should therefore be directed to these products in the hope of achieving equilibrium with local consumption.

Unless I am missing something, there are only three ways to earn more with a given product. First, one can try to increase the quantity produced. Second, one can try to improve the quality. And third, one can try to stop the market price from falling. The second and third methods often go together, and all three are applicable in Kabylia.

Increasing the production of figs and olives should be considered, and it is also worth considering whether complementary products such as cherries and carobs might also prove viable. Both experiments have been tried in the commune of Port-Gueydon, and these should be treated as constructive examples.

In 1938, the commune assisted in the planting of 1,000 new saplings. This year, 10,000 to 15,000 trees will be planted. And all of this has been done without supplementary appropriations. The

Société Indigène de Prévoyance guaranteed loans to pay for the planting, and shoots were delivered to the fellahin (peasants) who asked for them. They had the opportunity to observe the quality and yield of these plants in test groves planted on communal land.

As with the fig tree, which is planted when saplings are two years old but does not yield fruit until it is five, the fellahin will, for the first five years, pay only interest on the minimal capital required to purchase the saplings. The interest rate is only 4 percent. After five years, the tree begins to produce figs, and the Kabyle peasant then has five additional years to pay off the loan.

To give you an idea of the return on investment, I should add that even if only one-third of the new trees become productive (which is a conservative estimate), the fellah will still come out ahead, and his success will have cost the state practically nothing. No comment is necessary. If this experiment is aggressively expanded to other areas, the results will soon be obvious.

When it comes to improving existing products and raising their market price, the task is immense. Here I will discuss only the key elements: setting up drying houses to improve the quality of dried figs and establishing cooperatives to produce olive oil. The traditional methods of Kabyle agriculture are not well suited to increasing yields. The usual pruning of olive trees, which resembles an amputation, the unsystematic removal of saplings, the racks used to dry figs on rooftops or under carob trees that leave the fruit vulnerable to parasites—none of these things enhances the quality of the final product.

Many communes have therefore experimented with drying houses. The most instructive of these experiments were carried out in Azazga and Sidi-Aïch. In Azazga, the rational methods implemented by state-sponsored advisers increased the price of the final product by 120 percent the first year and 80 percent the second year. In Sidi-Aïch, figs from the drying house sold for an average of 260 francs per quintal compared with 190 for native figs. In Azazga, 120 fellahin participated in the experiment by bringing their figs to the drying house, and they earned 180,000 francs in revenue. After initial resistance, the majority of fellahin therefore embraced the innovation. A private cooperative is planned in Temda, to be managed by the producers themselves. This is likely to be an image of Kabylia's future.

Setting up olive oil cooperatives has been a more difficult process. Some administrators oppose the idea owing to opposition from lowland settlers, who prefer to purchase olives at low cost rather than high-priced olive oil. In addition, middlemen and brokers would stand to lose under the new system and therefore oppose it. But Kabyle farmers need credit, for which they turn to these same middlemen, who lend them money in exchange for a claim on their future production. This obstacle can be overcome, however, if olive oil cooperatives are associated with a credit union that could fill the role of middleman. A final argument that is sometimes heard insists that Kabyle farmers would nevertheless continue to turn to other middlemen for needed cash. But this is an argument that is raised against every proposed innovation, and it has always been indefensible.

Unfortunately, the methods used by Kabyle farmers allow them to harvest olives only once every two years. A more rational system needs to be imposed, and it is certain that output would then be close to doubled. European factories have increased their yield, but the methods they use ensure that the oil produced has an acid content of at least 1.5 to 2 percent and therefore has an unpleasant taste.

———

Finally, these policies can succeed only if additional steps are taken to deal with other issues. Housing, for example, could be based on the model established by the Loucheur Law.[1] The beneficiaries of housing assistance could contribute by providing land, labor, and materials (nearly every Kabyle owns a plot of land). There are also grounds for reconsidering the way in which communal revenues are shared between the European and native population and for asking Europeans to make the necessary sacrifices.

These policies would revive the real Kabylia. The dreadful misery of the region would at last be alleviated and compensated. I know that money is needed to achieve these goals, but I say again, let us begin by making better use of the money that has already been appropriated, because what is missing is not so much money, perhaps, as commitment. Nothing great has ever been accomplished without courage and lucidity. If these policies are to succeed, it is not enough to hope for improvement now and then: our determination must be constant and focused. I know that many will object "that there is no reason why the colony and colonists should pay." And I agree. So let us not wait for the colonists to act, because we cannot be sure that they will. But if you say that it is up to metropolitan France to step in, then I agree with you for two reasons. First, the status quo proves that a system that divorces Algeria from France is bad for France. And second, when the interests of Algeria and France coincide, then you can be sure that hearts and minds will soon follow.

1. The Loucheur Law of July 13, 1928, provided state aid for low-cost housing.—*Trans.*

Conclusion

This text will conclude my survey of conditions in Kabylia, and I would like to make sure that it will serve well the cause of the Kabylian people—the only cause it was intended to serve. I have nothing more to say about the misery of Kabylia or about its causes and cures. I would have preferred to end with what I have already written, without adding useless words to a set of facts that should be able to speak for themselves. But preferable though it might have been to say nothing, the misery of the Kabyles was so awful that it had to be talked about. And for the same reason, these essays might fail to achieve their purpose if I did not dispose of certain facile criticisms by way of conclusion.

I will not mince words. These days, it seems that one is not a good Frenchman if one speaks of the misery of a French territory. I must say that it is hard to know nowadays what one must do to be a good Frenchman. So many people, of so many different kinds, boast of this title, and among them there are so many mediocre minds and self-promoters, that one can easily go wrong. Still, it is possible to know what it means to be a just person. And my prejudice is that France is best represented and defended by acts of justice.

Some will object, "Be careful, foreigners will use what you say." But those who might use what I say are already guilty in the eyes of the world of cynicism and cruelty. And if France can be defended against them, it will be done not only with cannons but also with the freedom that we still possess to say what we think and to do our modest part to repair injustice.

My role, moreover, is not to point a misleading finger of blame. I have no liking for the prosecutorial role. And even if I did like that role, many things would prevent me from filling it. I am only too well aware of the distress that the economic crisis has brought to Kabylia to level absurd charges at some of its victims. But I am also too well aware that many generous initiatives have met with resistance, even those backed by the highest authorities. And I am aware, finally, of the way in which the best of intentions can be distorted when applied in practice.

What I have tried to say is that, despite what people have wanted to do and have done for Kabylia, their efforts have addressed only small pieces of the problem while leaving the heart of the matter untouched. I write these words not for a party but for human beings. And if I wanted to describe the results of my investigation, I would say that the point is not to say to people "Look at what you have done to Kabylia" but rather "Look at what you have not done for Kabylia."

Against charity, limited experiments, good intentions, and idle words, weigh in the balance famine and filth, loneliness and despair, and you will see whether the former outweigh the latter. If by some miracle the 600 deputies of France could travel the same itinerary of hopelessness that I did, the Kabyle cause would take a great leap forward. Indeed, there is always progress when a political problem is replaced by a human problem. If a lucid, focused policy is formulated to attack Kabylian poverty and bring the region back to life, then we will be the first to praise an effort of which we cannot be proud today.

———————

I cannot refrain from saying one last word about the region I have just visited. This will be my real conclusion. Of long days poisoned by horrifying sights in the midst of an incomparable natural environment, what I remember is not just the desperate hours but also certain nights when I thought I had achieved a profound understanding of this country and its people.

I recall, for instance, one night, in front of the Zaouïa of Koukou,[1] a few of us were wandering in a cemetery of gray stones and contemplating the night as it fell across the valley. At that hour, no longer day but not yet night, I was aware of no difference between me and the others who had sought refuge there in search of a part of themselves. But I had no choice but to become aware of that difference a few hours later, when everyone should have sat down to eat.

It was there that I discovered the meaning of my investigation. If there is any conceivable excuse for the colonial conquest, it has to lie in helping the conquered peoples to retain their distinctive personality. And if we French have any duty here, it is to allow one of the proudest and most humane peoples in this world to keep faith with itself and its destiny.

I do not think I am mistaken when I say that the destiny of this people is to work and to contemplate, and in so doing to teach lessons in wisdom to the anxious conquerors that we French have become. Let us learn, at least, to beg pardon for our feverish need of power, the natural bent of mediocre people, by taking upon ourselves the burdens and needs of a wiser people, so as to deliver it unto its profound grandeur.

1. Koukou was a Berber kingdom in northern Algeria. The Zaouïa was its general assembly.—*Trans.*

CRISIS IN ALGERIA

Articles published in *Combat* in May 1945.

Crisis in Algeria

When one looks at the recent disturbances in North Africa, it is wise to avoid two extremes. One is to describe as tragic a situation that is merely serious. The other is to ignore the grave difficulties with which Algeria is grappling today.

To adopt the first attitude would be to play into the hands of interests out to persuade the government to take repressive measures that would be not only inhumane but also impolitic. To adopt the second would be to continue to widen the gap that for so many years has separated the metropolis from its African territories. In either case, one would be opting for a shortsighted policy as harmful to French interests as to Arab ones.

The survey that follows is the fruit of a three-week visit to Algeria, and its only ambition is to reduce the incredible ignorance of the metropolis in regard to North African affairs. I tried to be as objective as possible as I traveled more than 1,500 miles along the Algerian coast as well as inland to the limits of the southern territories.

I visited not only cities but also the most remote douars, and I listened to the opinions and firsthand accounts of bureaucrats and native farmers, of colonists and Arab militants. A good policy is first of all a well-informed policy. Of course this survey is just that: a survey. But if the facts I report are not new, they have been checked. I therefore hope that they can be of some use to those charged with coming up with a policy that can save Algeria from spinning out of control.

————

Before going into detail about the North African crisis, however, it may be useful to dispose of a certain number of prejudices. To begin with, I want to remind people in France of the fact that Algeria exists. By that I mean that it exists independent of France and that its problems have their own peculiar texture and scale. Hence one cannot resolve those problems by following the metropolitan example.

One simple fact will suffice to illustrate what I mean. All French schoolchildren learn that Algeria, which falls under the jurisdiction of the Ministry of the Interior, consists of three *départements*. Administratively, that is true. In fact, however, those three *départements* are the size of forty typical French *départements* and have a population equivalent to twelve. So the metropolitan bureaucracy thinks it has done a great deal when it sends 2,000 tons of grain to Algeria, but that amounts to exactly one day's consumption of the country's eight million inhabitants. The next day they have to start all over again.

————

As for the political dimension, I want to point out that the Arab people also exist. By that I mean that they aren't the wretched, faceless mob in which Westerners see nothing worth respecting or defending. On the contrary, they are a people of impressive traditions, whose virtues are eminently clear to anyone willing to approach them without prejudice.

These people are not inferior except in regard to the conditions in which they must live, and we have as much to learn from them as they from us. Too many French people in Algeria and elsewhere imagine the Arabs as a shapeless mass without interests. One more fact will set them straight.

In the most remote douars, 500 miles from the coast, I was surprised to hear the name of M. Wladimir d'Ormesson mentioned. The reason for this was that, a few weeks ago, our colleague published an article on the Algerian question that Muslims deemed to be ill-informed and insulting. I'm not sure that the journalist for the *Figaro* will be glad to know how quickly he made a reputation for himself in Arab lands, but it does tell us a great deal about the political awakening of the Muslim masses. Finally, if I point out one more fact of which too many French people are ignorant—namely, that hundreds of thousands of Arabs have spent the past two years fighting for the liberation of France—I will have earned the right to move on to other matters.

In any case, all this should teach us not to prejudge anything about Algeria and to refrain from repeating clichés. In a sense, the French have to conquer Algeria a second time. To sum up my impressions from my visit, I should say that this second conquest will not be as easy as the first. In North Africa as in France, we need to invent new recipes and come up with new ways of doing things if we want the future to make sense to us.

The Algeria of 1945 is enduring the same economic and political crisis it has always endured, though never before to this degree. In this lovely country, now glorious with spring blossoms and sunshine, people suffering from hunger are demanding justice. We cannot remain indifferent to their suffering, because we have experienced it ourselves.

Rather than respond with condemnations, let us try to understand the reasons for their demands and invoke on their behalf the same democratic principles that we claim for ourselves. My goal in the remaining articles of this series is to support this effort simply by supplying objective information.

––––––

P.S. This article was complete when an evening paper appeared with an article accusing Ferhat Abbas, president of the "Friends of the Manifesto," of having personally organized the Algerian disturbances. This article was obviously written in Paris on the basis of fragmentary information. Nevertheless, it is unacceptable to make such a serious accusation on the basis of such flimsy evidence. There is much to be said for and against Ferhat Abbas and his party. We will in fact be discussing him. But French journalists must recognize that a problem this serious cannot be resolved by intemperate appeals for blind repression.

Famine in Algeria

The most obvious crisis afflicting Algeria is an economic one.

Algeria already shows unambiguous signs of this to the attentive visitor. The leading taverns serve drinks in cut-off bottles with the edges filed down. Hotels give you wire coat hangers. Bombed-out stores have fallen beams in their windows rather than glass. In private homes it is not uncommon for the bulb used to light the dining room to be moved to the bedroom after dinner. There is a shortage of manufactured goods, no doubt because Algeria has no industry, but above all there is an import crisis. We will be looking at its effects.

The news that must be shouted from the rooftops is that most Algerians are experiencing a famine. This is the reason for the serious disturbances we have heard about, and this is what needs fixing. The population of Algeria is nine million in round numbers. Of these nine million, eight million are Arabo-Berbers, compared with a million Europeans. Most of the Arab population is scattered throughout the vast countryside in *douars,* which French colonial administrations have combined into mixed villages. The basic diet of the Arabs consists of grains (wheat or barley), consumed in the form of couscous or flatbread. For want of grain, millions of Arabs are suffering from hunger.

Famine is still a dreadful scourge in Algeria, where harvests are as capricious as the rainfall. In normal times, however, the reserves maintained by the French administration made up the shortfall caused by drought. There are no longer any reserves in Algeria, because they were transferred to the metropolis for the benefit of the Germans. The Algerian people were therefore at the mercy of a bad harvest.

———

That misfortune has happened. Let me mention just one fact to give you an idea of how bad it was. Throughout the high plateaus of Algeria, there has been no rain since January. These vast fields are covered with wheat no higher than the poppies that stretch off to the horizon. The land, covered with cracks like a lava flow, is so dry that double teams had to be used for the spring planting. The plow tears at the flaky, powdery soil incapable of holding the sown seed. The harvest expected for this season will be worse than the last, which was already disastrous.

———

I beg the reader's indulgence if I cite some figures. Normally, Algeria requires some 18 million quintals of grain. As a general rule, its production is roughly equal to its consumption: for instance, the 1935–1936 harvest of all grains combined was 17,371,000 quintals. Last season's total was barely 8,715,000 quintals, however, which is just 40 percent of normal needs. This year's forecasts are even more pessimistic, with a maximum expectation of roughly six million quintals.

The drought is not the only reason for this terrifying shortage. The acreage devoted to grain has decreased, because there is less seed and also because fodder is not taxed, so that certain heedless landowners chose to grow it rather than essential grains. Certain temporary technical difficulties also play a part: deteriorating equipment (a plow blade that used to cost 20 francs now goes for 500), fuel rationing, and labor shortages due to the military mobilizations. What is more, demand for grain has increased owing to rationing of other foods. Without help from the outside world, it is clear, therefore, that Algeria cannot feed its population from its own soil.

————

To witness the consequences of this famine is enough to break your heart. The administration was obliged to reduce the grain allowance to 7.5 kilograms per person per month (farmworkers receive 18 kilograms from their employers, but they are a minority). That works out to 250 grams per day, which is not much for people whose only staple is grain.

Yet even this famine ration could not be honored in the majority of cases. In Kabylia, in the Ouarsensis, in the South Oranais, and in the Aurès (to take widely separated regions), four to five kilograms per month was the most that could be distributed, which comes to 130 to 150 grams per person per day.

Is it clear what that means? Is it clear that in a country where sky and land are invitations to happiness, this means that millions of people are suffering from hunger? On every road one sees haggard people in rags. Traveling around the country, one sees fields dug up and raked over in bizarre ways, because an entire douar has come to scratch the soil for a bitter but edible root called *talrouda,* which can be made into a porridge that is at least filling if not nourishing.

The reader may be wondering what can be done. To be sure, the problem is a difficult one. But there is not a minute to waste, and no one's interests can be spared, if we want to save these wretched people and stop hungry masses egged on by criminal madmen from resuming the savage massacre in Sétif. In my next article I will indicate what injustices must be ended and what emergency measures must be taken in the economic sphere.

Ships and Justice

What can we do for the millions of Algerians who are suffering from hunger? It doesn't take exceptional political lucidity to observe that only a policy of massive imports can change the situation.

The government has just announced that a million quintals of wheat will be distributed in Algeria. That is good. Bear in mind, however, that this amount is enough to meet the needs of only about a month's consumption. There is no way to avoid sending the same quantity of grain to Algeria next month and the month after that. The import problem has thus not been solved, and it will continue to require the utmost energy.

I am by no means unaware of the difficulty of the undertaking. To restore the situation, feed the Arab population properly, and eliminate the black market, Algeria will need to import 12 million quintals. That amounts to 240 shiploads of 5,000 tons each. Given the state in which the war has left us, everyone understands what that means. But given the urgency of the situation, it must also be recognized that we cannot allow anything to stand in our way and must, if necessary, demand that the world provide the necessary ships. When millions of people are suffering from hunger, it becomes everybody's business.

When we have done this, however, we still will not have done everything we can, because the gravity of the Algerian affair does not stem solely from the fact that the Arabs are hungry. It also stems from the fact that their hunger is unjust. Hence it is not enough to give Algeria the grain it needs; that grain must also be distributed equitably. I would have preferred not to write this, but it is a fact that the distribution is not equitable.

————

For proof of this assertion, consider first the fact that in this country, where grain is almost as scarce as gold, it can still be found on the black market. In most of the villages I visited, it was possible to buy grain not at the official price of 540 francs per quintal but at an underground price ranging from 7,000 to 16,000 francs per quintal.[1] The black market is supplied with wheat siphoned from official supplies by thoughtless colonists and native overlords.

Furthermore, the grain that is delivered to distribution points is not distributed equally. The caïdship, that most harmful institution, continues to wreak havoc. The caïds, who act in a sense as stewards representing the French administration, have all too often been entrusted with the task of overseeing distributions of grain, and the methods used are often highly idiosyncratic.

The distributions carried out by the French administration itself are inadequate but generally honest. Those carried out by the caïds are generally unfair, governed by self-interest and favoritism.

Finally, to save the most painful point for last, the ration distributed to natives throughout Algeria is inferior to that distributed to Europeans. This is the case officially, since a European is entitled to 300 grams per day, compared with 250 for an Arab.

1. To give an idea of prices, wheat at 10,000 francs per quintal meant that a kilo of bread cost about 120 francs. An Arab worker's weekly salary averaged about 60 francs.

Unofficially, the situation is even worse, since the typical Arab receives only 100 to 150 grams, as I mentioned earlier.

The people of Algeria, animated by a sure and instinctive sense of justice, might perhaps accept the need for such severe rationing in principle. But they do not accept (as they made clear to me) the idea that because it was necessary to limit rations, only Arab rations should have been reduced. People who have not been stingy with their blood in this war are justified in thinking that others should not be stingy with their bread.

This unequal treatment, together with various other abuses, has created a political malaise, which I will deal with in forthcoming articles. But within the context of the economic problem that concerns me now, it is further poisoning an already grave situation, and it is adding to the suffering of the natives a bitterness that could have been avoided.

To quell the cruelest of hungers and heal inflamed hearts: that is the task we face today. Hundreds of freighters filled with grain and two or three measures of strict equality: this is what millions of people are asking of us, and perhaps this will help to make it clear why we must try to understand them before we judge them.

II

The Political Malaise

As grave and urgent as the economic privation from which North Africa is suffering is, it cannot by itself account for the Algerian political crisis. If we discussed the famine first, it was because hunger is the first priority. But when we have done everything that needs to be done to feed the Algerian population, we still will only have scratched the surface. Or, to put it another way, we will still, at long last, need to come up with a policy for North Africa.

Far be it from me to try to formulate a definitive policy for North Africa in the space of two or three articles. This would please no one, and truth would not be served. But our Algerian policy is so distorted by prejudice and ignorance that to offer an objective account based on accurate information is already to render an important service. That is what I propose to do.

————

I read in a morning newspaper that 80 percent of the Arabs wished to become French citizens. In contrast, I would sum up the current state of Algerian policy by saying that, indeed, Arabs used to want to become citizens but no longer do. When you have hoped for something for a long time and your hopes are dashed, you avert your eyes, and your erstwhile desire disappears. That is what has happened to the indigenous peoples of Algeria, and the primary responsibility for this is ours.

French colonial doctrine in Algeria since the conquest has not been notable for its coherence. I shall spare the reader the history of its fluctuations, from the notion of an Arab kingdom favored by the Second Empire to that of assimilation. In theory, it was the idea of assimilation that triumphed in the end. For the past 50 years or so, France's avowed goal in North Africa was gradually to open the way to French citizenship for all Arabs. Let it be said at once that this idea remained theoretical. In Algeria itself, the policy of assimilation met with unremitting hostility, primarily on the part of the most influential colonizers.

———

There exists a whole arsenal of arguments—some of them apparently convincing at first sight—which have until now sufficed to keep Algeria immobilized in the political situation we have described.

I won't discuss these arguments. But it is clear that on this issue as on others, someday a choice will have to be made. France had to state clearly whether, on the one hand, it considered Algeria to be a conquered land whose subjects, stripped of all rights and burdened with additional duties, would be forced to live in absolute dependence on us, or, on the other hand, it attributed to its democratic principles a value universal enough to be able to extend them to populations for which it had accepted responsibility.

France, to its credit, chose, and having chosen, it was obliged, if words were to mean anything, to follow the logic of its decision to the end. Special interests opposed this venture and tried to turn back the clock. But time inexorably marches on, and people evolve.

No historical situation is ever permanent. If you are unwilling to change quickly enough, you lose control of the situation.

————

Because French policy in Algeria ignored these elementary truths, it was always 20 years behind the actual situation. An example will help to make this clear.

In 1936, the Blum-Viollette Plan marked a first step toward a policy of assimilation after 17 years of stagnation. It was by no means revolutionary. It would have granted civil rights and voting status to roughly 60,000 Muslims. This relatively modest plan aroused immense hopes among the Arabs. Virtually the entire Arab population, represented by the Algerian Congress, indicated its approval. But leading colonists, banded together in the Financial Delegations and the Association of Mayors of Algeria, mounted a counteroffensive powerful enough to ensure that the plan was never even presented to the chambers.

————

The dashing of this great hope naturally led to a very radical disaffection. Now the French government is proposing that Algeria accept the ordinance of March 7, 1944, whose electoral provisions more or less emulate those of the Blum-Viollette Plan.

If this ordinance were really enforced, it would give the vote to roughly 80,000 Muslims. It would also eliminate the exceptional legal status of Arabs, a goal for which North African democrats have fought for years. In effect, Arabs were not subject to the same penal code or even the same courts as Frenchmen. Special tribunals, more severe in their punishments and more summary in their procedures, kept Arabs in a permanent state of subjection. The new ordinance has eliminated that abuse, and that is a very good thing.

———

Arab opinion, much dampened by all that has taken place, remains reserved and wary, however, despite all the good things in the new plan. The problem is quite simply that time marches on. The fall of France was followed by a loss of French prestige. The 1942 landing brought Arabs into contact with other nations and spurred them to make comparisons. Finally, one cannot ignore the fact that the Pan-Arab Federation is a constant temptation for the people of North Africa, whose misery only adds to all their other grievances. As a result of all this, a plan that would have been welcomed enthusiastically in 1936 and would have solved a great many problems is today met only with wariness. Once again we are late.

Peoples generally aspire to political rights only in order to set themselves on the road to social progress. The Arab people wanted the right to vote because they knew that, with it, and through the free exercise of democracy, they could eliminate the injustices that are poisoning the political climate of Algeria today. They knew that they could eliminate inequalities in wages and pensions, as well as more scandalous inequalities in military allowances and, in a more general sense, everything that helped to perpetuate their inferior status. But the Arabs seem to have lost their faith in democracy, of which they were offered only a caricature. They hope to achieve by other means a goal that has never changed: an improvement in their condition.

That is why, to believe my sample, Arab opinion is in its majority indifferent or hostile to the policy of assimilation. This is most unfortunate. But before deciding what ought to be done to improve the situation, we must have a clear sense of what the political climate in Algeria is today.

Arabs today face any number of possibilities, and since, historically, every aspiration of a people finds political expression, Muslims have lately found themselves drawn to a remarkable figure, Ferhat Abbas, and his "Friends of the Manifesto" party. In my next article, I will discuss this important movement, the most important and novel to have appeared in Algeria since the early days of the conquest.

The Party of the Manifesto

I said in my last article that a substantial number of North African natives, having given up on the policy of assimilation but not yet won over by pure nationalism, had turned to a new party, the "Friends of the Manifesto." I therefore think it would be useful to make French people familiar with this party, which, like it or not, has to be reckoned with.

The leader of this movement is Ferhat Abbas, a native of Sétif, a university graduate with a degree in pharmacy, and, before the war, one of the staunchest proponents of the assimilation policy. At that time he edited a newspaper, *L'Entente,* which defended the Blum-Viollette Plan and called for the establishment in Algeria of a democratic political system in which Arabs would enjoy rights corresponding to their duties.

Today, Abbas, like many of his coreligionists, has turned his back on assimilation. His newspaper, *Egalité,* whose editor Aziz Kessous is a socialist as well a former proponent of assimilation, is calling for Algeria to be recognized as a nation linked to France by ties of federalism. Ferhat Abbas is fifty years old. He is undeniably a product of French culture. The epigraph of his first book was a quotation from Pascal. This was no accident. He is in fact a man in the Pascalian spirit, combining logic and passion with some considerable success. The following thought is very much in the French style: "France will be free and strong by dint of our freedoms and our strengths." Ferhat Abbas owes his style to our culture, as he is well aware. Even his humor bears the French stamp, as is evident from the following classified ad, which appeared in upper-case characters in *Egalité:* "Exchange one hundred feudal lords of all races for 100,000 French teachers and technicians."

This cultivated and independent man has evolved along with his people, and he has set forth their aspirations in a manifesto that was published on February 10, 1943, and accepted by General Catroux as a basis for discussion.

———

What does the manifesto say? In truth, taken on its own terms, the text limits itself to a detailed critique of French policy in North Africa and to the assertion of a principle. That principle, which takes note of the failure of the assimilation policy, is that there is a need to recognize an Algerian nation linked to France but distinctive in character. According to the manifesto, "it is now clear to everyone that this assimilation policy is an *unattainable reality* [my italics] and a dangerous instrument designed to serve the interests of the colonization."

Building on this principle, the manifesto asks that Algeria be given its own constitution in order to ensure that Algerians will enjoy full democratic rights and parliamentary representation. An appendix added to the manifesto on May 26, 1943, and two more recent texts from April and May 1945, further flesh out this position. The amended manifesto calls for recognition, an end to hostilities, and an Algerian state with its own constitution, to be drafted by a constituent assembly elected by universal suffrage of all people residing in Algeria.

The general government would then cease to be a bureaucratic agency and become a true government, with top positions equally divided between French and Arab ministers.

As for the assembly, the "Friends of the Manifesto" were aware that any proposal for strictly proportional representation would have met with hostility in France, since with eight Arabs to every Frenchman in the population, the assembly would then become a de facto Arab parliament. As a result, they agreed that their constitution should allow for 50 percent Muslim representatives and 50 percent Europeans. Hoping to spare French sensibilities, they accepted the idea that the powers of the assembly would be limited to administrative, social, financial, and economic matters, leaving all problems of external security, military organization, and diplomacy to the central government in Paris. Of course, this basic text is accompanied by social demands, all of which are aimed at bringing the fullest possible democracy to Arab politics. I believe, however, that I have accurately summarized the gist of the document and have not distorted the ideas of the Friends of the Manifesto.

———

In any case, a substantial number of Muslims have rallied around these ideas and the man who represents them. Ferhat Abbas has united a diverse group of individuals and movements, including the Oulémas, a group of Muslim intellectuals who preach a rationalist reform of Islam and who were until recently proponents of assimilation, along with socialist militants. It is also quite clear that elements of the Algerian Popular Party, an Arab nationalist group that was dissolved in 1936 but has illegally continued to propagandize in favor of Algerian separatism, have joined the Friends of the Manifesto, which they may regard as a good platform for further action.

It is possible that it was this latter group that involved the Friends of the Manifesto in the recent disturbances. From a direct source, however, I know that Ferhat Abbas is too keen a political mind to have advised or desired such excesses, which he knew would only reinforce the politics of reaction in Algeria. The man who wrote "Not one African will die for Hitler" has given sufficient guarantees in this regard.

The reader may think that he would be inclined to favor the program I have just laid out. Whatever his opinions, however, he should know that this program exists and that it has profoundly influenced Arab political aspirations.

Although the French government has decided not to follow General Catroux's lead in giving tentative approval to the manifesto, it may have noticed that the entire political basis of the document rested on the fact that it judged assimilation to be "an unattainable reality." The government might then have concluded that it would suffice to make that reality attainable in order to undermine the argument of the Friends of the Manifesto. Instead, it preferred to respond with prison sentences and repression— stupidity pure and simple.

13

Conclusion

The French, whose confidence was shaken for a time, have since lost interest in Algerian affairs. In the ensuing period of relative calm, articles have been published in various newspapers arguing that the political crisis is not that serious or widespread and is simply the work of a handful of professional agitators. Not that these articles are distinguished by careful documentation or objectivity. One describes the recently arrested president of the "Friends of the Manifesto" as the father of the Algerian Popular Party, which has been led for many years by Messali Hadj, who was also arrested. Another treats the Oulémas as a nationalist political organization when it is in fact a reformist religious group, which actually supported a policy of assimilation until 1938.

No one has anything to gain from these hasty and ill-informed articles, nor from the far-fetched studies that have appeared elsewhere. To be sure, the Algerian massacre would not have occurred had there been no professional agitators. Nevertheless, those agitators would not have had much effect if they had not been able to take advantage of a political crisis from which it would be pointless and dangerous to avert one's eyes.

This political crisis, which has been going on for many years, did not miraculously disappear overnight. Indeed, it has grown more severe, and all the information coming from Algeria suggests that it has lately been enveloped by a climate of hatred and distrust that nothing can alleviate. The massacres of Guelma and Sétif have provoked deep indignation and revulsion in the French of Algeria. The subsequent repression has sown fear and hostility in the Arab masses. In this climate, the likelihood that a firm but democratic policy can succeed has diminished.

But that is not a reason to despair. The Ministry of National Economy has envisioned resupply measures that, if continued, should be enough to recover from a disastrous economic situation. But the government must maintain and extend the ordinance of March 7, 1944, in order to prove to the Arab masses that no ill feeling will ever interfere with its desire to export to Algeria the democratic regime that the French enjoy at home. But what we need to export is not speeches but actions. If we want to save North Africa, we must show the world our determination to give it the best of our laws and the most just of our leaders. We must demonstrate our resolve and keep to it regardless of the circumstances or attacks in the press. We must convince ourselves that in North Africa as elsewhere, we will preserve nothing that is French unless we preserve justice as well.

As we have seen, words like these will not please everyone. They cannot easily overcome blindness and prejudice. But we continue to believe that this is a reasonable and moderate approach. The world today is dripping with hatred everywhere. Violence, force, massacre, and tumult darken an atmosphere from which we thought the poison had been drained. Whatever we can do in service of the truth—French truth and human truth—we must do to counter this hatred. Whatever it costs, we must bring peace to nations that have too long been torn and tormented by all that they have suffered. Let us at least try not to add to the bitterness that exists in Algeria. Only the infinite force of justice can help us to reconquer Algeria and its inhabitants.

14

Letter to an Algerian Militant[1]

My dear Kessous,

I found your letters upon returning from my vacation, and I am afraid that my approval will arrive very late. Yet I need to let you know how I feel. Believe me when I tell you that Algeria is where I hurt at this moment, as others feel pain in their lungs. And since August 20, I have been on the edge of despair.

———

Only a person who knows nothing of the human heart can think that the French of Algeria can now forget the massacres in Philippeville. Conversely, only a madman can believe that repression, once unleashed, can induce the Arab masses to trust and respect France. So we now find ourselves pitted against one another, with each side determined to inflict as much pain as possible on the other, inexpiably. This thought is unbearable to me, and it poisons my days.

1. When the rebellion broke out, Mr. Aziz Kessous, an Algeria Socialist and former member of the Party of the Manifesto, had the idea of publishing a newspaper, *Communauté Algérienne*, the aim of which was to transcend the twin fanaticisms that plague Algeria today and thus help to create a truly free community. This letter appeared in the first issue of the paper on October 1, 1955.

And yet you and I, who are so alike, who share the same culture and the same hopes, who have been brothers for so long, joined in the love we both feel for our country, know that we are not enemies. We know that we could live happily together on this land, which is our land—because it is ours, and because I can no more imagine it without you and your brothers than you can separate it from me and my kind.

You said it very well, better than I will say it: we are condemned to live together. The French of Algeria—who, I thank you for pointing out, are not all wealthy bloodsuckers—have been in Algeria more than a century and number more than a million. That alone is enough to distinguish the Algerian problem from the problems of Tunisia and Morocco, where the French settlement is relatively small and recent. The "French reality" can never be eliminated from Algeria, and the dream that the French will suddenly disappear is childish. By the same token, there is no reason why nine million Arabs should be forgotten on their own soil. The dream that the Arabs can be forever negated, silenced, and subjugated is equally insane. The French are attached to Algerian soil by roots too old and deep to think of tearing them up. But this does not give the French the right to cut the roots of Arab life and culture. All my life, I have defended the idea that our country stands in need of far-reaching reform (and as you well know, I paid the price in the form of exile). No one believed me, and people continued to pursue the dream of power, which always believes that it is eternal and always forgets that history does not stop. Today reform is more necessary than ever. Your proposals would constitute an indispensable first step and should be implemented without delay, provided they are not drowned beforehand in either French or Arab blood.

But I know from experience that to say these things today is to venture into a no-man's-land between hostile armies. It is to preach the folly of war as bullets fly. Bloodshed may sometimes lead to progress, but more often it brings only greater barbarity and misery. He who pours his heart into such a plea can expect only laughter and the din of the battlefield in reply. And yet someone must say these things, and since you propose to try, I cannot let you take such an insane and necessary step without standing with you in fraternal solidarity.

Of course, the crucial thing is to leave room for whatever dialogue may still be possible, no matter how limited. It is to defuse tensions, no matter how tenuous and fleeting the respite may be. To that end, each of us must preach peace to his own side. The inexcusable massacres of French civilians will lead to other equally stupid attacks on Arabs and Arab property. It is as if madmen inflamed by rage found themselves locked in a forced marriage from which no exit was possible and therefore decided on mutual suicide. Forced to live together but incapable of uniting their lives, they chose joint death as the lesser evil. Because each side's excesses reinforce the reasons—and the excesses—of the other, the deadly storm now lashing our country will only grow until the destruction is general. Constant escalation has caused the blaze to spread, and soon Algeria will be reduced to ruin and littered with corpses. No force or power on earth will be capable of putting the country back together in this century.

The escalation must therefore stop, and it is our duty as Arabs and Frenchmen who refuse to let go of one another's hands to stop it. We Frenchmen must fight to stop collective repression and to ensure that French law remains generous and clear. We must fight to remind our compatriots of their errors and of the obligations of a great nation, which cannot respond to a xenophobic massacre with a similar paroxysm of rage if it wishes to retain its stature in the world. And we must fight, finally, to hasten the adoption of necessary and crucial reforms, which will once more set the Franco-Arab community of Algeria on the road to the future. Meanwhile, you Arabs must tirelessly explain to your own people that when terrorism kills civilians, it not only raises doubts about the political maturity of people capable of such acts but also reinforces anti-Arab factions, validates their arguments, and silences French liberals who might be capable of propounding and promoting a compromise solution.

I will be told, as you will be told, that the time for compromise is over and that the goal now must be to wage war and win. But you and I both know that there will be no real winners in this war and that both now and in the future we will always have to live together on the same soil. We know that our destinies are so closely intertwined that any action by one side will bring a riposte by the other, crime leading to crime and insanity responding to madness. If one side abstains, however, the other will wither. If you Arab democrats fail in your effort to restore peace, then we French liberals will inevitably fail in our own efforts. And if we flag in our duty, your wan words will vanish in the wind and flames of a pitiless war.

That is why I am with you one hundred percent, my dear Kessous. I wish you, I wish us, good luck. I want to believe with all my heart that peace will dawn on our fields, our mountains, and our shores, and that Arabs and Frenchmen, reconciled in liberty and justice, will try hard to forget the bloodshed that divides them today. On that day, we who are together exiles in hatred and despair will together regain our native land.

ALGERIA TORN

This series of articles appeared in *L'Express* between October 1955 and January 1956. It summed up arguments and positions expressed in the same magazine between July 1955 and February 1956.

15

The Missing

The Palais Bourbon[1] has been a crowded place over the past three days, but one party was missing: Algeria. French deputies, gathered to vote on a policy for Algeria, spent five sessions failing to reach a decision on three agenda items. Meanwhile, the government initially displayed a fierce determination not to settle anything before the Assembly voted. Then, no less firmly, it insisted on a vote of confidence for its lack of a policy from deputies who had to look up the meaning of the words they were using in a dictionary. Clearly, France continues to get nowhere. In the meantime, however, Algeria is dying.

It would be nice if it were not necessary to attack the people who are struggling mightily with our institutions, as Gilliatt struggled with the octopus.[2] But this is no time for indulgence. For Algeria, bloodshed is the order of the day. The Assembly's three votes will add to the death toll. While the deputies waste their time in useless talk, people are dying alone, their throats slit and their screams unheard. The deputies consult their dictionaries while Algerians take up arms.

Who has given a thought to the ordeal of reservists called to battle, to the solitude of the French in Algeria, or to the anguish

1. Where the French National Assembly meets.—*Trans.*
2. In Victor Hugo's novel *The Toilers of the Sea.*—*Trans.*

of the Arab people? Algeria is not France. It is not even Algeria. It is a neglected, faraway land populated by incomprehensible natives, cumbersome soldiers, and exotic Frenchmen, all bathed in a mist of blood. The fact that it is missing from the discussion distresses those who remember the place and were sorry to see it abandoned; others want to talk about it, but only if it says nothing in its own behalf.

Were recent lessons learned therefore of no avail? Solutions that might have been considered before August 20 are now out of the question. The elections that were once necessary and possible are now unimaginable without a cease-fire. The gulf between the two populations has widened. Extremists outdo one another in destruction. The worst can be avoided only if the government immediately adopts a firm, clear policy. But no! The opposition attacks the government and in the same breath congratulates the official who carries out the government's orders. Thus impotent moderation continues to serve the extremes, and our history is still an insane dialogue between paralytics and epileptics.

One chance remains, however. The contending forces could meet for a frank final discussion. This is the only possible way to overcome some of the barriers that separate the French of Algeria from both the Arabs and the people of metropolitan France. And if the dictionary and the legislative agenda prevent our politicians from agreeing to such a meeting, let us at least pave the way as far as we possibly can. I would like to do my part in the coming days, despite the difficulty right now of working out a position that is fair to everyone. In the end, though, what does it matter if we cannot find the words, or stumble over them, if those words can, however briefly, bring exiled Algeria back among us, with all its wounds, so that we can at least agree on an agenda of which we need not be ashamed?

16

The Roundtable

Political problems cannot be resolved with psychology. Without psychology, however, problems will certainly become more complicated. In Algeria, bloodshed has driven people apart. Let us not make things worse through stupidity and blindness. Not all the French in Algeria are bloodthirsty brutes, and not all Arabs are fanatical mass killers. Metropolitan France is not populated solely by passive officials and generals nostalgic for battle. Similarly, Algeria is not France, though many people, superb in their ignorance, continue to insist that it is. Yet it is home to more than a million French men and women, as is all too often forgotten in certain quarters. These simplifications only exacerbate the problem. What is more, one justifies the other, and together their consequences are lethal. Day after day these simplifications prove, in a sort of reductio ad absurdum, that in Algeria the French and the Arabs are condemned either to live together or to die together.

Of course, if despair becomes overwhelming, one may choose to die. Yet to dive into the water in order to avoid the rain would be unforgivable, as would dying because one sought to survive. That is why the idea of a roundtable around which would gather representatives of all tendencies, from colonizers to Arab nationalists, still seems valid to me. It is not good for people to live apart, or isolated in factions. It is not good for people to spend too much time nursing their hatred or feelings of humiliation, or even contemplating their dreams. The world today is one in which the enemy is invisible. The fight is abstract, and there is consequently nothing to clarify or alleviate it. To see and hear the other can therefore give meaning to the combat and just possibly make it unnecessary. The roundtable will be a time for accepting responsibility.

This will not happen, however, unless the meeting is fair to all sides and open. It is not in our power to ensure fairness. On principle I would not leave it up to the government to do so. But the fact is that the matter is today in the government's hands, and that makes us anxious. In any case, the roundtable must not be part of some new round of useless bargaining intended to maintain in power men who evidently chose to go into politics in order to avoid making policy.

That leaves the matter of publicity, about which we can do something. I will therefore devote several articles to the simplifications I alluded to above, explaining to each party to the talks the reasoning of its adversaries. Objectivity does not mean neutrality, however. The effort to understand makes sense only if there is a prospect of justifying a decision in the end. I will therefore conclude by taking a stand. And let me say at once that it will be a stand against despair, because in Algeria today, despair means war.

17

A Clear Conscience

The gulf between metropolitan France and the French of Algeria has never been wider. To consider the metropole first, it is as if the long-overdue indictment of France's policy of colonization has been extended to all the French living in Algeria. If you read certain newspapers, you get the impression that Algeria is a land of a million whip-wielding, cigar-chomping colonists driving around in Cadillacs.

This is a dangerous cliché. To heap scorn on a million of our fellow Frenchmen or quietly disdain them, indiscriminately blaming all for the sins of a few, can only hinder rather than encourage the progress that everyone claims to want, because such scorn inevitably affects the attitudes of the French settlers. Indeed, at the moment a majority of them believe that metropolitan France has stabbed them in the back—and I ask my metropolitan readers to measure the gravity of this situation.

In a separate article I will try to show the settlers that their judgment is incorrect. Nevertheless, it exists, and the settlers, united by a bitter sense of abandonment, cling to it except when dreaming of criminal repression or stunning surrender. What we need most in Algeria today, however, is a body of liberal opinion capable of moving quickly toward a solution, before the country is bathed in blood. In any case, this need should force us to make the distinctions essential to a just apportionment of the respective responsibilities of colony and metropole.

Those distinctions are in fact quite easy to make. Eighty percent of the French settlers are not colonists but workers and small businessmen. The standard of living of the workers, though superior to that of the Arabs, is inferior to that of workers in the metropole. Two examples will suffice to make this clear. The minimum wage is set at a level below that found in the poorest parts of France. The father of a family with three children receives not quite 7,200 francs in social benefits, compared with 19,000 in France. Those are your colonial profiteers.

Yet these same ordinary people are the first victims of the present situation. They are not the ones placing ads in the papers, looking to buy property in Provence or apartments in Paris. They were born in Algeria and will die there, and their one hope is that they will not die in terror or be massacred in the pit of some mine. Must these hardworking Frenchmen, who live in isolated rural towns and villages, be sacrificed to expiate the immense sins of French colonization? Those who think so should first say as much and then, in my view, go offer themselves up as expiatory victims. It is too easy to allow others to be sacrificed, and if the French of Algeria bear their share of responsibility, the French of France must not forget theirs either.

Who in fact has wrecked every reform proposal of the last 30 years, if not a parliament elected by the French? Who closed their ears to the cries of Arab misery? Who remained indifferent to the repression of 1945, if not the vast majority of the French press? And finally, who, if not France, waited with a revoltingly clear conscience until Algeria was bleeding before taking note of the fact that the country even existed?

If the French of Algeria nursed their prejudices, was it not with the blessing of the metropole? And wouldn't the French standard of living, as inadequate as it was, not have been worse but for the misery of millions of Arabs? All of France battened on the hunger of the Arabs—that is the truth. The only innocents in this affair were the young men who were sent into battle.

The true responsibility for the current disaster rests primarily with a series of French governments, backed by the comfortable indifference of the press and public opinion and supported by the complacency of lawmakers. In any case, they are more guilty than the hundreds of thousands of French workers who scrape by in Algeria on their miserable wages, who responded three times in 30 years to the call to take up arms on behalf of the metropole, and who are rewarded today by the contempt of the very people they helped. They are more guilty than the Jewish populations that have been caught for years between French anti-Semitism and Arab distrust and who today find themselves forced by French indifference to seek refuge in another country.

Let us admit, therefore, once and for all, that the fault here is collective, but let us not draw from this fact the conclusion that expiation is necessary. Such a conclusion would become repugnant the moment others were called upon to pay the price. In politics, moreover, nothing is ever expiated. Errors can be repaired, and justice can be done. The Arabs are due a major reparation, in my opinion, a stunning reparation. But it must come from France as a whole, not from the blood of French men and women living in Algeria. Say this loud and clear and I know that those settlers will overcome their prejudices and participate in the construction of a new Algeria.

18

The True Surrender

I said that the metropole could help to narrow the gulf between it and Algeria by renouncing demagogic simplifications. But the French of Algeria can help too by restraining their bitterness and overcoming their prejudices.

Mutual recrimination and hateful attacks change nothing of the reality that grips us all. Like it or not, the French of Algeria face a choice. They must choose between the politics of reconquest and the politics of reform. The first option means war and far-reaching repression. For some French settlers, however, the second option would mean surrender. This is not just a simplification; it is an error, and it could become a fatal error.

For a nation like France, the ultimate form of surrender is called injustice. In Algeria, it was a surrender to injustice that preceded the Arab rebellion and that explains why it occurred, though without justifying its excesses.

To favor reform, moreover, is not—as some odiously maintain—to approve of the massacre of civilian populations, which remains a crime. It is rather to seek to prevent the shedding of innocent blood, be it Arab or French. It is of course reprehensible to play down the massacres of French men and women in order to focus attention solely on the excesses of the repression. Yet no one is entitled to condemn the massacres unless he or she unreservedly rejects those excesses. On this point, at least, it seems to me that agreement is essential, precisely because it is so painful.

The crux of the matter, ultimately, is that to reject reform is the real surrender. It is a reflex of fear as much as anger, and a denial of reality. The French in Algeria know better than anyone that the policy of assimilation has failed—first because it was never really tried, and second because the Arab people have retained their own character, which is not identical to ours.

Two peoples, tied to each other by circumstances, may choose to enter into a partnership or to destroy each other. The choice in Algeria is a choice not between surrender and reconquest but between a marriage of convenience and a deadly marriage of two xenophobias.

If French Algeria refuses to recognize the Arab character, it will work against its own interests. To reject reform would be tantamount to rejecting the Arab people, who have their rights, and their more lucid militants, who do not deny that we have ours, in favor of feudal Egypt and Franco's Spain, which have only appetites. That would be the real surrender, and I cannot believe that the French of Algeria, whom I know to be realists, do not recognize the gravity of the stakes.

Instead of relentlessly attacking the failures of the metropole, it would be better to help it work toward a solution that takes Algerian realities into account. Those realities include the misery and deracination of the Arabs on the one hand and the security of the French settlers on the other. If the settlers prefer to wait for a plan concocted by four bored politicians between two campaign tours to become the charter of their misfortune, they can choose moral secession.

But if they wish to preserve the essential, to build an Algerian community in a peaceful and just Algeria, a community that will allow both French settlers and Arabs to embark on the road to a shared future, then they should join us, speak out, and propose ideas with the confidence that comes of true strength. And they should also know—I want to stress this point—that it is not France that holds their destiny in hand but French Algeria that is today deciding not only its own fate but also the fate of France.

19

The Adversary's Reasons

Before coming, if not to the solutions of the Algerian problem, then at least to the method that might make them possible, I must first say a word to Arab militants. I must ask them, too, not to simplify things and not to make Algeria's future impossible.

I know that, from my side of the divide, those militants are used to hearing more encouraging words. If I were an Algerian fighter and received assurances of unconditional support from the French side, I would of course eagerly welcome that support. But being French by birth and since 1940 by deliberate choice, I will remain French until others are willing to cease being German or Russian. I will therefore speak in accordance with what I am. My only hope is that any Arab militants who read me will at least consider the arguments of a person who for 20 years, and long before their cause was discovered by Paris, defended their right to justice, and did so on Algerian soil, virtually alone.

I urge them first to distinguish carefully between those who support the Algerian cause because they want to see their own country surrender on this as on other fronts and those who demand reparations for the Algerian people because they want France to demonstrate that grandeur is not incompatible with justice. Of the friendship of the former, I will say only that it has already demonstrated its inconstancy. The others, who are and have been more reliable, surely deserve not to have their difficult task rendered impossible by mass bloodshed or blind intransigence.

The massacres of civilians must first be condemned by the Arab movement, just as we French liberals condemn the massacres of the repression. Otherwise, the relative notions of innocence and guilt that guide our action would disappear in the confusion of generalized criminality, which obeys the logic of total war. Since August 20, the only innocents in Algeria are the dead, whatever camp they may come from. Leaving them aside, what remains is two types of guilt, one of which has existed for a very long time, the other of which is of more recent vintage.

To be sure, this is the law of history. When the oppressed take up arms in the name of justice, they take a step toward injustice. But how far they go in that direction varies, and although the law of history is what it is, there is also a law of the intellect, which dictates that although one must never cease to demand justice for the oppressed, there are limits beyond which one cannot approve of injustice committed in their name. The massacre of civilians, in addition to reviving the forces of oppression, exceeded those limits, and it is urgent that everyone recognize this clearly. On this point, I have a proposal to make concerning the future, and I will do so in a moment.

The question of intransigence remains. The farsighted militants of the North African movement, those who know that the Arab future depends on rapid access to the conditions of modern life for Muslim peoples, at times seem to have been outstripped by another movement, which is blind to the vast material needs of the ever-increasing masses and dreams of a pan-Islamism that is more readily imagined in Cairo than in the face of historical reality. This dream, which in itself is worthy of respect, has no immediate future, however. It is therefore dangerous. Whatever one thinks of technological civilization, it alone, for all its weaknesses, is capable of bringing a decent life to the underdeveloped countries of the world. Materially speaking, the salvation of the East will come not from the East but from the West, which will then itself draw nourishment from the civilization of the East. Tunisian workers saw this clearly and supported Bourguiba and the UGTT rather than Salah ben Youssef.

The French to whom I referred earlier cannot in any case support the wing of the Arab movement that is extremist in its actions and retrograde in its doctrine. They do not regard Egypt as qualified to speak of freedom and justice or Spain to preach democracy. They are in favor of an Arab identity for Algeria, not an Egyptian identity. And they will not become champions of Nasser and his Stalin tanks or of Franco as a prophet of Islam and the dollar. In short, they cannot become enemies of their own convictions or their own country.

The Arab identity will be recognized by the French identity, but for that to happen it is necessary for France to exist. That is why we who are today demanding that the Arab identity be recognized also continue to defend the true identity of France, that of a people who in their vast majority, and alone among the great nations of the world, have the courage to recognize the reasons of their adversary, which is currently engaged in a struggle to the death with France. This country, which it is repugnant to call racist because of the exploits of a minority, today offers the Arab people their best chance of a future, and it does so in spite of its errors, the price of which has in any case been far too many humiliations.

20

November 1

Algeria's future is not yet totally compromised. As I wrote in a previous article, if each party to the conflict makes an effort to examine the reasons of its adversary, an entente may at last become possible. As a step toward that inevitable agreement, I would like to set forth its conditions and limits. On this anniversary, however, let me first say that there would be no point to making the effort if an intensification of the hatred and killing were to place the desired result beyond the realm of possibility.

If the two Algerian populations were to seek to massacre each other in a paroxysm of xenophobic hatred, nothing anyone could say would be able to bring peace to Algeria, and no reform would be able to resurrect the country from its ruins. Those who call for such massacres, no matter which camp they come from and no matter what argument or folly drives them, are in fact calling for their own destruction. The blind souls who are demanding widespread repression are in fact condemning innocent French people to death. And by the same token, those who courageously avail themselves of microphones far from the scene to call for murder are laying the groundwork for the massacre of Arab populations.

On this point at least, Franco-Arab solidarity is complete, and the time has come to recognize this. This solidarity can lead to either a dreadful fraternity of pointless deaths or an alliance of the living in a common task. But no one, dead or alive, will be able to escape the choice.

It therefore seems to me that no one, French or Arab, can possibly want to embrace the blood-soaked logic of total war. No one on either side should refuse to limit the conflict in ways that will prevent it from degenerating. I therefore propose that both camps commit themselves publicly and simultaneously to a policy of not harming civilian populations, no matter what the circumstances. For the time being, such a commitment would not change the situation. Its purpose would simply be to make the conflict less implacable and to save innocent lives.

What can be done to make this simultaneous declaration a reality? For obvious reasons, it would be desirable if the initiative came from France. The governor general of Algeria or the French government itself could take this step without making any fundamental concessions. But it is also possible that for purely political reasons, both parties might prefer a less politicized intervention. In that case, the initiative might be taken by the religious leaders of the three major denominations in Algeria. They would not need to obtain or negotiate an agreement, which would lie outside their competence, and could simply issue an unambiguous call for a simultaneous declaration on this one specific issue, which would then bind the parties in the future without inciting a pointless quarrel about the past.

It is not enough to say that such a commitment would facilitate the search for a solution. Without it, no solution is possible. There is an important difference between a war of destruction and a simple armed divorce: the former leads to nothing but further destruction, whereas the latter can end in reconciliation.

If there is to be reconciliation, the public commitment for which we are calling is a necessary but not sufficient first step. To reject it out of hand would be tantamount to admitting publicly that one places little value on one's own people and, furthermore, that the only goal is pointless and unlimited destruction. I do not see how either party to the conflict can refuse to make a pure and simple humanitarian statement that would be clear in its terms and significant in its consequences. Each party can do so, moreover, without giving up any of its legitimate grievances. Yet no one can shirk this obligation without revealing his true designs, which can then be taken into account.

A Truce for Civilians

Not a day goes by without terrible news from Algeria arriving by mail, newspaper, and even telephone. Calls for help—nay, cries for help—ring out everywhere. In one morning I received a letter from an Arab schoolteacher whose village witnessed the summary execution of several men by firing squad and a call from a friend on behalf of French workers killed and mutilated at their workplace. And one has to live with this news in a Paris buried under snow and filth, each day more oppressive than the last.

If only the escalation could be stopped. What is the point of each side brandishing its victims against those of the other? All the dead belong to the same tragic family, whose members are now slitting one another's throats in the dead of night, the blind killing the blind without being able to see who they are.

The tragedy has not left everyone in tears, moreover. Some exult about it, albeit from afar. They deliver sermons, but beneath their grave mien the cry is always the same: "Hit harder! See how cruel that fellow is! Gouge his eyes out!" Unfortunately, if there is anyone left in Algeria who has not kept pace with the escalating killing and vengeance, he will soon catch up. Before long, Algeria will be populated exclusively by murderers and victims. Only the dead will be innocent.

There is a priority of violence: I know that. The long years of colonialist violence explain the violence of the rebellion. But that justification is applicable only to the armed rebellion. How can one condemn the excesses of the repression if one ignores or says nothing about the extremes of the rebellion? And conversely, how can one be outraged by the massacres of French prisoners if one tolerates the execution of Arabs without trial? Each side uses the crimes of the other to justify its own. By this logic, the only possible outcome is interminable destruction.

"Everyone must choose sides," shout the haters. But I have chosen. I have chosen a Just Algeria, where French and Arabs may associate freely. And I want Arab militants to preserve the justice of their cause by condemning the massacre of civilians, just as I want the French to protect their rights and their future by openly condemning the massacres of the repression.

When it becomes clear that neither side is capable of such an effort, or of the lucidity that would allow them to perceive their common interests, and when it becomes clear that France, caught between its money machine and its propaganda machine, is incapable of developing a policy that is both realistic and generous, then and only then will we give up hope. But these things are not yet clear, and we must fight to the end against the consequences of hatred.

Time is of the essence. Every day that goes by destroys a little more of Algeria and promises years of additional misery for its population. Each death drives the two populations a little farther apart. Tomorrow, they will face each other not across an abyss but over a common grave. Whatever government is chosen a few weeks from now to deal with the Algerian problem, there is a danger that by then there will be no way out of the current impasse.

It is therefore up to the French of Algeria to take the initiative themselves. They are afraid of Paris, I know, and they are not always wrong to be afraid. But what are they doing in the meantime? What are they proposing? If they do nothing, others will do for them, and what grounds would they then have to complain? I am told that some of them, suddenly enlightened, have chosen to support Poujade.[1] I am not yet prepared to believe that they would choose a course tantamount to suicide. Algeria needs creative thinking, not shopworn slogans. The country is dying, poisoned by hatred and injustice. It can save itself only by overcoming its hatred and with a surfeit of creative energy.

———

It is therefore necessary to appeal once again to the French of Algeria: "While defending your homes and your families, you must find the additional strength to recognize what is just in the cause of your adversaries and to condemn what is unjust in the repression. Be the first to propose ways of saving Algeria and establishing fair cooperation among the various sons and daughters of the same soil." And Arab militants must be addressed in similar terms. While fighting for their cause, they must at last disavow the murder of innocents and propose their own plan for the future.

And all must be enjoined to seek a truce. A truce until solutions can be found, a truce in which both sides will refrain from killing civilians. Until the accuser sets an example, all accusations are

1. Pierre Poujade (1920–2003), a right-wing populist politician and leader of the Poujadiste movement.—*Trans.*

useless. French friends and Arab friends, I urge you to respond to one of the last appeals for an Algeria that is truly free and peaceful and soon prosperous and inventive. There is no other solution. There is no solution but the one we are proposing. Apart from it, there is only death and destruction. Movements are forming everywhere, I know, and courageous people, both Arab and French, are regrouping. Join them. Aid them with all your might. They are Algeria's last and only hope.

22

The Party of Truce

The time is approaching when the Algerian problem will require a solution, yet no solution is in sight. Apparently, nobody has a real plan. People are fighting about the method and the means, while no one pays any attention to the ends.

People tell me that some in the Arab movement are proposing a form of independence that would sooner or later result in the eviction of the French from Algeria. But the French have been in Algeria long enough and in large enough numbers that they, too, constitute a people who cannot tell others what to do but by the same token cannot be made to do anything without their consent.

Meanwhile, fanatics among the colonists break windows to cries of "Repression!" and postpone any possibility of reform until after the victory. In practical terms, this is tantamount, morally speaking, to suppression of the Arab population, whose identity and rights cannot be denied.

These are the doctrines of total war. Neither can be called a constructive solution. A more fruitful proposal, to my mind, is the one approved yesterday by the Socialist Congress, which said that there can be no unilateral negotiation in Algeria. Indeed, the two words are contradictory. To have a negotiation, each party must take the other party's rights into account and concede something for the sake of peace.

Two things make this confrontation difficult. The first is the absence of any Algerian political structure, which colonization prevented, whereas the protectorates in Tunisia and Morocco at least paid lip service to the indigenous state. The second stems from the absence of any clearly defined French position as a result of our political instability. In a clash between passions, no one can define his own position in relation to that of his adversary. Escalation then becomes the only form of expression.

We cannot create a new political structure in Algeria overnight. That is precisely the problem that needs to be resolved. But the French government could clarify its position by recognizing the need to negotiate with duly elected interlocutors and to state clearly what it can and cannot accept. Today, what the government cannot accept is clear. Succinctly stated, the situation is this: yes to an Arab identity in Algeria, no to an Egyptian identity. With the government tottering, there is no majority in France in favor of the strange coalition that has formed against us, uniting Madrid, Budapest, and Cairo. On this point, the no must be firm. But the stronger that no is, the more steadfast must be the commitment to treat the Arab people justly and to conclude an agreement to which they can freely assent.

This cannot happen unless French opinion in Algeria evolves considerably. The bloody marriage of terrorism and repression is no help in this regard, nor is the escalation of hateful demagoguery in both camps. Those who are still capable of dialogue must come together. The French who believe that a French presence in Algeria can coexist with an Arab presence in a freely chosen regime, who believe that such coexistence will restore justice to all Algerian communities without exception, and who are sure that only such a regime can save the Algerian people from death today and misery tomorrow must at last shoulder their responsibilities and preach peace so that dialogue might once again be possible. Their first duty is to insist with all their strength that a truce be established at once in regard to civilians.

———

Once such a truce is achieved, the rest might follow. In Algeria it is not only necessary for individuals to come together, it is also possible. A clear and steady path toward justice, a union of differences, and confidence in the possibilities of the future—all of us, French and Arabs alike, should be able to get behind a party based on these principles. The party of truce would then become Algeria itself. What is at stake is life itself. I experience the current situation as akin to the war in Spain and the defeat of 1940—events that changed the men and women of my generation and forced them to recognize the uselessness of the political nostrums that had previously guided them. If, through some concatenation of misfortunes, the unwitting coalition of two blind enemies were to result in the death, in one way or another, of the Algeria for which we hope, then we would have to take stock of our impotence and reconsider all our commitments and positions, for the whole meaning of history will have changed for us.

The hope remains, however, that we will be capable of building the kind of future we have in mind. The difficult and exalting task of nurturing that hope lies with the French of Algeria, the French of France, and the Arab people themselves.

23

Call for a Civilian Truce in Algeria

Ladies and gentlemen,[1]

Despite the precautions that had to be taken to protect this meeting, and despite the difficulties we face, I come before you tonight not to divide but to unite. That is my most ardent wish. It is not the least of my disappointments, to put it mildly, that the deck seems to be stacked against this wish, and that a man, a writer, who has devoted a part of his life to the service of Algeria, is in danger of being denied the opportunity to speak even before anyone knows what he has to say. But this only confirms the urgency of the effort we must make for peace. This meeting was supposed to demonstrate that there is still a chance for dialogue. It was supposed to prevent the general feeling of discouragement from ending in passive acceptance of the worst.

In using the word "dialogue," I mean to signal that I did not come here to give a standard lecture. The fact is that, as things now stand, I haven't the heart for that. But I thought it possible, and even considered it my duty, to come before you to issue a simple appeal to your humanity, which in one respect at least might be able to calm tempers and bring together a majority of Algerians,

1. This is the text of a speech delivered in Algiers on January 22, 1956.

both French and Arab, without asking them to relinquish any of their convictions. This appeal, which has been sponsored by the committee that organized this meeting, is addressed to both camps and calls on them to accept a truce that would apply exclusively to innocent civilians.

My only purpose today is therefore to argue in favor of this initiative. I will try to be brief.

Let me say first—and I cannot emphasize this enough—that by its very nature this appeal falls outside the realm of politics. If it were otherwise, I would not be qualified to discuss it. I am not a politician. My passions and preferences summon me to places other than this podium. I am here only under the pressure of the situation and the way I sometimes conceive of my profession as a writer. On the substance of the Algerian question, I may have more doubts than certitudes to express, given the pace of events and the growing suspicions on both sides. My only qualification to speak about this issue is that I have experienced Algeria's misfortune as a personal tragedy. Nor can I rejoice in any death, no matter whose it is. For twenty years I have used the feeble means available to me to help bring harmony between our two peoples. To my preaching in favor of reconciliation, history has responded in cruel fashion: the two peoples I love are today locked in mortal combat. The look of consternation on my face is no doubt a cause for laughter. But I myself am not inclined to laugh. In the face of such failure, my only conceivable concern is to spare my country any unnecessary suffering.

I should add that the people who took the initiative to support this appeal were also not acting on political grounds. Some of them, representing different religious faiths, were responding to a high call and felt a duty to humanity. Others were people whose professions and predilections do not normally involve them in public affairs. Most do work that is useful to the community, work that suffices to fill their lives. They might have remained on the sidelines, like so many others, counting the attacks while occasionally lamenting the losses in the most melancholic tones. But they felt that the work of building, teaching, and creating—generous, life-enhancing work—cannot continue in a land overwhelmed by hatred and drenched in blood. Their decision to do something—a decision from which numerous consequences and commitments flow—gives them only one right: to demand that others think about what they are proposing.

Finally, I should say that our goal is not to win your political support. If we tried to get to the heart of the issue, we would risk failing to win the agreement we need. We may differ about the necessary solutions and even about the means to achieve them. To rehearse yet again positions that have already been stated and distorted a hundred times would for now merely add to the insults and enmities under which the country has been struggling and suffocating.

But at least one thing unites us all: namely, love of the land we share, and distress. Distress in the face of a future that becomes a little more inaccessible each day, distress at the threat of a rotten war and an economic crisis that is already serious and steadily getting worse, and which threatens to get so bad that recovery will take many years.

It is this distress that we want to address, even, and indeed especially, in the presence of those who have already chosen sides. For even among the most determined of those partisans, those engaged in the heat of the battle, there remain some, I am sure, who are not resigned to murder and hatred and who dream of a happy Algeria.

It is to that unresigned part of each of you, French or Arab, that we appeal tonight. Without dredging up yet again the errors of the past, and anxious only for the future, it is to those who have not resigned themselves to seeing this great country broken in two that we want to say today that it is still possible to come to an agreement on two simple points: first, to come together, and second, to save human lives and thus bring about a climate more favorable to reasonable discussion. The modesty of this goal is deliberate, yet it is important enough, in my opinion, to deserve your broad approval.

What do we want? We want the Arab movement and the French authorities, without entering into contact with each other or making any other commitment, to declare simultaneously that as long as the troubles continue, civilian populations will at all times be respected and protected. Why? The first reason, on which I will not insist, is, as I said earlier, one of simple humanity. However old and deep the roots of the Algerian tragedy are, one fact remains: no cause justifies the deaths of innocent people. Throughout history, human beings, though incapable of banning war itself, have tried to limit its effects. As horrible and repugnant as the two world wars were, organizations offering aid and assistance were able to illuminate the darkness with rays of pity that made it impossible to give up hope in mankind altogether. The need for such help seems all the more urgent in what appears in many ways to be a fratricidal struggle, an obscure combat in which lethal force makes no distinction between men and women or soldiers and workers. Even if our initiative were to save only one innocent life, it would still be justified.

But it is also justified on other grounds. Although Algeria's future looks bleak, it is not yet entirely compromised. If everyone, Arab as well as French, were to make an effort to think about his adversary's justifications, then a useful discussion might at least begin. But if each side in Algeria accuses the other of starting the conflict and both go at each other in a kind of xenophobic frenzy, then any chance of agreement will be definitively drowned in blood. For us, the greatest source of distress is the thought that we may be headed toward such horrors. But that cannot and must not happen until those of us, Arab and French, who reject nihilism's folly and destructiveness have issued a final appeal to reason.

In one sense, as reason clearly shows, Franco-Arab solidarity is inevitable, in life as in death, in destruction as in hope. The hideous face of this solidarity can be seen in the infernal dialectic according to which what kills one side also kills the other. Each camp blames the other, justifying its own violence in terms of its adversary's. The endless dispute over who committed the first wrong becomes meaningless. Because two populations so similar and yet so different, and each worthy of respect, have not been able to live together, they are condemned to die together, with rage in their hearts.

There is also a community of hope, however, and it is this that justifies our appeal. This community accepts the fact that certain realities cannot be changed. Sharing this land are a million Frenchmen who have been settled here for more than a century, millions of Muslims, both Arab and Berber, who have been here for many centuries, and any number of strong and vibrant religious communities. These people must live together where history has placed them, at a crossroads of commerce and civilizations. They can do so if only they are willing to take a few steps toward one another for a free and open debate. Our differences should then help us rather than drive us apart. In this as in other things, I, for one, believe only in differences, not uniformity, because differences are the roots without which the tree of liberty withers and the sap of creation and civilization dries up. Yet we remain frozen in one another's presence as if stricken with a paralysis from which only sudden spasms of violence can liberate us. This is because the struggle has taken on an implacable character that arouses on both sides irrepressible rage and passions that can be slaked only by escalation.

"No further discussion is possible." This is the attitude that kills any chance of a future and makes life impossible. What follows is blind struggle, in which the French decide to ignore the Arabs, even if they know deep down that the Arab demand for dignity is justified, and the Arabs decide to ignore the French, even though they know deep down that the French of Algeria also have a right to security and dignity on the land we all share. Steeped in bitterness and hatred, each side finds it impossible to listen to the other. Every proposal, no matter what its nature, is greeted with suspicion and immediately twisted into a form that renders it useless. Little by little we become caught in a web of old and new accusations, acts of vengeance, and endless bitterness, as in an ancient family quarrel in which grievances accumulate generation after generation to the point where not even the most upright and humane judge can sort things out. It becomes difficult to imagine how such an affair can end, and the hope of a Franco-Arab partnership in a peaceful and creative Algeria fades with each passing day.

If we want to keep a little of this hope alive until substantive debate can begin, and if we want to make sure that with an effort of mutual understanding that debate has some hope of altering the status quo, then we must act to change the nature of the struggle itself. For now we are too hamstrung by the scope of the tragedy and the complexity of the passions that have been unleashed to hope for an immediate cessation of hostilities. Any attempt to obtain this would require purely political moves that for the time being might lead to still further division.

We can act, however, on what is odious about the conflict itself. We can propose not to change the present situation but simply to renounce what makes it unforgivable, namely, the slaughter of the innocent. The fact that such a meeting would bring together French and Arabs equally committed to avoiding irreparable damage and irreversible misery would create a real opportunity to intervene in both camps.

If our proposal has a chance of being accepted—and it does—we can not only save precious lives but also restore a climate that could lead to healthy debate not sidetracked by absurd ultimatums. We can lay the groundwork for a more just and nuanced understanding of the Algerian problem. If we can achieve just a small thaw on this one issue, then we can hope that someday it might be possible to chip away at the mass of hatreds and insane demands that currently block all progress. The initiative would then pass to the politicians, each of whom would have the right to defend his position and explain how it differs from the positions of others.

In any case, this is the narrow position on which we can, for starters, hope to come together. For the time being, any broader platform would only offer scope for additional disagreement. We must therefore be patient with ourselves.

As for the proposed action, of the utmost importance despite its limitations, I do not think that any Frenchman or Arab can, after mature reflection, possibly reject it. To understand why, it is enough to imagine what would happen if, despite all the precautions and restrictions with which we have surrounded this proposal, it were to fail. A definitive divorce would follow, destroying all hope and leading to misfortunes of which we have only the faintest idea at present. Our Arab friends, who courageously stand with us today in a no-man's-land in which we find ourselves menaced by both sides and who, being torn themselves, already find it so difficult to resist calls for escalation, will be forced to surrender to a fatalism that will snuff out any possibility of dialogue. Directly or indirectly, they will join the struggle, when they might have become artisans of peace. It is therefore in the interest of every Frenchman to help them overcome this fatalism.

By the same token, it is in the direct interest of every Arab moderate to help us overcome another fatalism. Because if this proposal fails and our lack of influence is demonstrated, the French liberals who think that French and Arab can coexist in Algeria, who believe that such coexistence will respect the rights of both groups, and who are certain that there is in any case no other way of saving the people of this country from misery—those French liberals will be silenced for good.

Then, instead of participating in the broader community of which they dream, they will be thrown back on the only existing community that supports them, namely, France. So we too, whether by silence or deliberate choice, will join the struggle. It is this evolution on both sides that we must fear, and that is what makes action so urgent. To explain why, I cannot speak for our Arab friends, but I am a witness to what may happen in France. Here, I am aware of Arab suspicion of any and all proposals, and by the same token I am aware, as you must be too, that in France similar doubts and suspicions are growing and are in danger of becoming permanent if the French, already surprised by the continuation of the war in the Rif after the return of the sultan and by the revival of guerrilla warfare in Tunisia, are forced by the spread of unrestrained warfare in Algeria to believe that the goal of the struggle is not simply justice for a people but furtherance of the ambitions of foreign powers at France's expense and to its ultimate ruin. If that were to happen, many in France would reason in the same way as the majority of Arabs if they were to lose all hope and submit to the inevitable. Their argument would be the following: "We are French. There is no reason why considering what is just in the cause of our adversaries should lead us to be unjust toward what deserves to survive and grow in France and its people. No one can expect us to applaud every form of nationalism except our own or to absolve every sin except the sins of France. Having been pushed to the limit, we must choose, and we cannot choose in favor of another country than our own."

If the adversary adopts a similar but opposite argument, our two peoples will separate once and for all, and Algeria will be left a field of ruins for many years to come, even though a little thought today could still turn things around and avoid the worst.

That is the danger we both face, the fatal dilemma we both confront. Either we succeed in joining together to limit the damage and thus encourage a more satisfactory evolution of the situation, or we fail to come together and persuade, and that failure will then color our whole future. That is what justifies our initiative and makes it so urgent. That is why my appeal will be more than insistent. If I had the power to give voice to the solitude and distress that each of us feels, I would speak to you in that voice. Speaking for myself, I have passionately loved this country, in which I was born and from which I have taken everything that I am, and among my friends who live here I have never distinguished by race. Although I have known and shared the misery that this country has not escaped, Algeria has nevertheless remained for me a land of happiness, energy, and creativity, and I cannot resign myself to seeing it become a land of unhappiness and hatred for years to come.

I know that many people are fascinated by the awfulness of history's great tragedies. Because of this, they remain transfixed, unable to decide what to do, simply waiting. They wait, and then one day the Gorgon devours them. I want to share with you my conviction that this spell can be broken, that this impotence is an illusion, and that sometimes, a strong heart, intelligence, and courage are enough to overcome fate. All it takes is will: will that is not blind but firm and deliberate.

We resign ourselves to fate too easily. We too readily believe that in the end there is no progress without bloodshed and that the strong advance at the expense of the weak. Such a fate may indeed exist, but men are not required to bow down before it or submit to its laws. Had they always done so, we would still be living in prehistoric times. In any event, men of culture and faith must never desert when historic battles are being waged, nor can they serve the forces of cruelty and inhumanity. Their role is to remain steadfast, to aid their fellow men against the forces of oppression, and to work on behalf of liberty against fatalism.

Only then is true progress possible. Only then can history innovate and create. Otherwise it repeats itself, like a bloody mouth from which an insane babble pours like vomit. We are still at the babbling stage, and yet the century holds the prospect of great things. We are in a knife fight, or something close to it, while the world is advancing at supersonic speed. On the same day that French papers ran the horrible story of our provincial quarrels, they also announced the Euratom treaty. Tomorrow, if only Europe could come to an agreement, a flood of riches would inundate the continent and spill over into Algeria, making our problems obsolete and our hatreds moot.

This is the future, so close and yet so hard to imagine, for which we must organize and strive. What is absurd and distressing about the tragedy we are experiencing is apparent in the fact that to enjoy the new global opportunities, we must band together in small numbers simply to demand that a handful of innocent victims be spared at one isolated place in the world, and nothing more. But since that is our task, obscure and thankless though it may be, we must confront it boldly so that we may one day deserve to live as free men, which is to say, as men who refuse both to engage in terror and to endure it.

The Maisonseul Affair

The next two pieces appeared in *Le Monde* in May and June 1956. On July 10, 1957, all charges against Jean de Maisonseul were dismissed.

24

Letter to *Le Monde*

Paris, May 28, 1956
To the Editor,

I am stunned to learn of the recent arrest in Algiers of my friend Jean de Maisonseul. I have thus far chosen to remain silent about the Algerian affair so as not to add to France's woes, and because in the end I did not approve of anything that was being said on the right or left. But it is impossible to remain silent in the face of such stupid and clumsy blunders, which strike directly at France's interests in Algeria. I have known Jean de Maisonseul for twenty years. During all that time he was never involved in politics. His only two passions were architecture and painting. Indeed, it was thanks to this great architect that the city of Orléansville rose from its ruins. In short, he was building Algeria while others were destroying it.

Quite recently, confronted with the tragedy of a country that he loved more than anything, he felt called upon to lend his name and support to my proposal for a civilian truce, the principle of which was approved by Messrs. Soustelle, Lacoste, and Mollet.[1]

---

1. Jacques Soustelle was governor general of Algeria from 1955 to 1956; Robert Lacoste was governor general of Algeria from 1956 to 1958; Guy Mollet was prime minister of France from 1956 to 1957.

This proposal did not seek to interpret or modify the present situation and was aimed solely at saving the lives of women, children, and the elderly, be they French or Arab. It was in no way intended as a basis for negotiation or even a simple "cease fire" and consisted entirely of a set of purely humanitarian measures that no one has yet had the impudence to criticize. The text of my appeal was made public, moreover, and to my knowledge no one has seen fit to declare its purpose scandalous or its intentions criminal. The "organization" mentioned in the agency dispatch is none other than the committee that sponsored this appeal, which has met with considerable encouragement despite the increasingly desperate situation. Our security services surely had no difficulty uncovering this "organization," whose existence was a matter of public notoriety.

Jean de Maisonseul was an active member of this committee. It is an abuse of language and power to use this fact as a pretext to accuse of him of relations with parties or factions that have never had anything to do with this committee, and still more of an abuse to accuse him of intending to negotiate a cease-fire or establish an independent Algerian republic. To read such imbecilities is simply flabbergasting.

I also see that Maisonseul is supposed to have joined the Fédération des Français Libéraux [Federation of French Liberals]. He is not the only one to have done so, and since this federation has, I am told, declared its intentions and registered its bylaws with the authorities, it is surely not a hanging offense to be a member. To arrest liberals solely because they belong to this group is to decree that in Algeria only the demonstrators of February 6 have the right to speak. If that is the case, I urge President Mollet to say whether or not he approves of this policy, which would be tantamount to charging anyone who does not insult the head of the French government with advocating surrender. I myself am firmly opposed to capitulation of all kinds, and I am no less opposed to the politics of the Algerian ultras, who to my mind represent a different sort of surrender, for which they bear a heavy responsibility. My position is exactly the same as Maisonseul's.

If his efforts on behalf of innocent French and Arab victims in Algeria were enough to get him indicted, then it is absolutely essential that I, too, should be arrested: I also took part in and will continue to take part in those efforts. Logically, it follows that the representatives of the Red Cross should also be arrested, along with Messrs. Mollet and Lacoste, who were aware of the project. Prime Minister Mollet in particular sent me a note of personal support for the committee's efforts just one month ago, a note that he himself characterized as warm. To be sure, his congratulations may well seem cold indeed in my friend's prison cell. Jean de Maisonseul may take consolation from the fact that he continues to enjoy the support of his friends throughout his shameful mistreatment. No one inside or outside the government is in a position to give lessons in patriotism to this courageous Frenchman. I can attest that he never failed in the loyalty he owed to his country, even, indeed especially, in what he did. By contrast, his arrest, and the crude and calculated misrepresentation of the reasons behind it, have truly sabotaged the French future in Algeria. The fellagha[2] leadership is no doubt laughing. And it is right to do so. These blind and brutal acts will not make up for the incredible failures of our diplomacy. They will instead add to the damage.

I nevertheless leave to the government responsibility for its policy and its police. The only thing that interests me is the liberation

2. Fellagha, from an Arabic word meaning literally "bandit" but also farmer, was the term applied to guerrillas who fought against France in Algeria.—*Trans.*

of Jean de Maisonseul. I will do everything in my power to alert the public and demand his release. It will then be necessary to seek reparations, because it would be intolerable to believe that an out-of-control police force can attack the honor of men of such quality with impunity.

––––––––

P.S. The latest reports say that Jean de Maisonseul is charged only with "imprudence" and that any action against him will be limited. I repeat: the alleged imprudent actions were in fact acts of civic courage that in no way harmed the interests of France and were known and approved in official circles. As for the limited charges, my indignation is all the greater, because there is unfortunately no limit to the damage being done to the reputation of a man who is beyond reproach, whose name has been subjected to the most revolting commentary on the radio and on the front pages of the newspapers. I repeat: it is incumbent on everyone free of partisan attachments to demand immediate reparations.

25

Govern!

A week after the arrest of Jean de Maisonseul, nothing remains of the charges lodged against him and promptly exploited by our treacherous elite. Robert Lacoste, the governor general, allegedly stated that the arrest had been made without his knowledge, while various government officials are said to be both apologetic and surprised. Clearly, emergency powers are not all they are cracked up to be. If there is no traitor and no conspiracy, then what remains of all the sound and fury of the past few weeks? Nothing but this—and I cannot write these words without rage and anger: my innocent friend is still in prison, where he is being held in secret, and his lawyers cannot communicate with him. In other words, it appears that the government of France is not in charge in Algeria, nor is Mr. Robert Lacoste, but rather persons unknown.

In fact, we knew this already. Algeria has long since become autonomous. French sovereignty has been challenged by a double secession. It must therefore be defended on two fronts or relinquished altogether. Anyone who refuses to fight on both fronts will end up shot in the back. The evidence is now clear, and it is certainly permissible to say that there is indeed a conspiracy in Algeria. But it is a conspiracy against the authority of the state and France's future. Some, employing the traditionally repugnant methods of the police, have tried to use intimidation and obfuscation to prove that all liberals are traitors so that France would stop counting generosity and justice among its arms. Our brilliant conspirators simply forgot that they were at the same time encouraging the fellagha by showing them that so many of the most respectable French citizens had made up their minds to surrender Algeria to the rebels. But I leave it to our ministers to draw the necessary conclusions and track down those responsible. My only interest is in the responsibility of the government itself.

I am willing to believe that the government had no part in the arbitrary arrest of Jean de Maisonseul, but the moment it became aware of that arrest and expressed its regret, it assumed responsibility for the arbitrary detention of an innocent man. From that moment on, the government has had no excuse, and it must bear full responsibility for every day, every night, and every hour of this scandalous imprisonment. To apologize for an injustice is nothing: there must be reparations. Banging on the table is not enough: one has to be obeyed. Otherwise we will be treated once again to the spectacle of a government without authority, dragged along by events it claims to control, deprived of both the energy of peace and the energy of war, and violated yet again at the very moment it proclaims its virtue.

Neither Jean de Maisonseul himself nor his friends can be satisfied with regrets expressed in a stage whisper. A man's freedom and reputation cannot be exchanged for condolences and regrets. These are carnal realities, matters of life and death. Between salvos of eloquence in the Chamber of Deputies and a man's honor, honor is the more urgent necessity, and more is at stake for France than in the dialogue between Dides and Cot.[1] Indeed, it is about time that this

---

1. Pierre Cot was a Socialist deputy. Jean Dides was a Poujadiste deputy who claimed that a "fifth column" in France was undermining the work of security forces in Algeria.

was said to men who spend so much of their time talking about restoring France's civic spirit. This is no doubt a matter of the utmost urgency, and I am surely not the last person to suffer from a certain French isolation, but it has to be said that this civic spirit vanished first from the precincts of government, where public service is in danger of losing its dignity. Passivity, indifference due to fatigue, and in some cases lack of character have given rise to a diminished conception of power, which neglects the innocent and indulges the guilty. The state may be legal, but it is legitimate only when it is the guarantor justice and the arbiter between the general interest and the liberty of the individual. If it ceases to be concerned with this, it loses its body, rots, and becomes nothing more than bureaucratized anarchy. And France is coming to resemble a worm that wriggles about in search of its head.

In light of all this, is the incredible news of the last few days really so surprising? Jean de Maisonseul, accused of a crime that officials privately acknowledge he did not commit, has been thrown in prison, while our yapping dogs, taking advantage of his helplessness, hasten to insult him. Meanwhile, France has delivered to Egypt and Syria arms whose effectiveness our young reservists, called to active duty, will sooner or later take the measure of. Here is a serious question, which I ask without polemical intent: Who has betrayed his country? The man who is suffering in prison for having sought, without ever failing in his duties, to spare innocent lives caught in the horrors of war? Or those who say with a straight face that they are executing contracts on which the profits will be paid in French blood? What is the difference between these officials and Cadet Maillot,[2] other than the fact

2. Henri Maillot was an officer cadet with the 57th Rifle Battalion who deserted in 1956 and took with him a truckload of weapons and munitions.

that Maillot did not take money for the weapons he delivered to the enemy? Yes, it's truly mind-boggling to learn these things, but it's also disheartening, and in the end one understands how such a government can allow a man it knows to be innocent to be deprived of his freedom. A government that wages war by arming its enemy is quite capable of deciding that the proper reward for innocence is prison and calumny. Weakness becomes a form of derangement, which can explain all these aberrations.

To prevent this weakness, this dangerous indifference to death, from establishing itself permanently in the top levels of government, we must remind our leaders of their responsibilities. I truly believe that only people unwilling to cede any of their rights will be steadfast in their duties. Hence it is all the more imperative that we surrender none of the rights of our innocent friend in prison. The continued detention of Jean de Maisonseul is a scandalous abuse of power, for which the government—and from this point on, the government alone—must be held responsible. Before appealing directly to the public and calling for protest by every means possible, I ask the government one last time to release Jean de Maisonseul immediately and to make public amends for his arrest.

ALGERIA 1958

26

Algeria 1958

For those who continue to ask me what future one may hope for in Algeria, I have written this brief note, in which I tried to limit myself to a minimum of verbiage and hew as close to reality as possible.

––––––––

If Arab demands as they stand today were entirely legitimate, Algeria would very likely be independent by now, with the approval of the French public. Like it or not, however, the French public continues to support the war, and even the Communists and their fellow-travelers limit themselves to Platonic protests. This is in part because Arab demands remain equivocal. This ambiguity, along with the confused responses it has provoked in successive French governments and in the country at large, explains the ambiguity of the French reaction and the omissions and uncertainties in which it has shrouded itself. If we are to devise a clear response, the first thing we must do is to be clear about what the Arab demands are.

––––––––

A. What is legitimate in the Arab demands? The Arabs are right, and everyone in France knows they are right, to denounce and reject:

1. Colonialism and its abuses, which are institutional.
2. The repeated falsehood of assimilation, which has been proposed forever but never achieved. This falsehood has compromised all progress based on colonialist institutions. In particular, the rigged elections of 1948 both exposed the lie and discouraged the Arab people once and for all. Until that date, all Arabs wanted to be French. After that date, a good many of them no longer did.
3. The evident injustice of the existing division of land and distribution of (subproletarian) income. Furthermore, these injustices have been irremediably aggravated by rapid population growth.
4. Psychological suffering: many French settlers have treated Arabs with contempt or neglect, and a series of stupid measures has fostered among the Arabs a sense of humiliation that is at the center of the current tragedy.

The events of 1945 should have been a warning: instead, the pitiless repression of the people of Constantine spurred the anti-French movement. The French authorities believed that the repression had ended the rebellion. In fact, it signaled the beginning.

There is no doubt that on all these points, which basically describe the historic status of the Algerian Arabs up to 1948, Arab demands are perfectly legitimate. The injustice from which the Arab people have suffered is linked to colonialism itself, to its history and administration. The French central government has never been able to enforce French law uniformly in its colonies. Finally, there is no question that the Algerian people deserve substantial reparations, both as a means of restoring their dignity and as a matter of justice.

B. What is illegitimate in the Arab demands:

The desire to regain a life of dignity and freedom, the total loss of confidence in any political solution backed by France, and the romanticism of some very young and politically unsophisticated insurgents have led certain Algerian fighters and their leaders to demand national independence. No matter how favorable one is to Arab demands, it must be recognized that to demand national independence for Algeria is a purely emotional response to the situation. There has never been an Algerian nation. The Jews, Turks, Greeks, Italians, and Berbers all have a claim to lead this virtual nation. At the moment, the Arabs themselves are not the only constituent of that nation. In particular, the French population is large enough, and it has been settled in the country long enough, to create a problem that has no historical precedent. The French of Algeria are themselves an indigenous population in the full sense of the word. Furthermore, a purely Arab Algeria would not be able to achieve economic independence, without which political independence is not real. French efforts in Algeria, however inadequate, have been sufficient that no other power is prepared to assume responsibility for the country at the present time. On this and related issues, I recommend the admirable book by Germaine Tillion.[1]

The Arabs claim to belong not to a nation[2] but to a spiritual or temporal Muslim empire of some sort. Spiritually, this empire exists, held together by Islam. But a no less important Christian

1. *Algeria 1957* (Paris: Editions de Minuit, 1957).
2. The Syrian "nation," only recently emerged from the French protectorate, melted like sugar in water into Nasser's Arab republic.

empire also exists, and no one is proposing to bring it back into temporal history. For the time being, the Arab empire exists not historically but only in the writings of Colonel Nasser, and there is no way it can become a reality without global upheavals that would lead in short order to World War III. The Algerian demand for national independence must in part be taken as a sign of this new Arab imperialism, which Egypt, overestimating its strength, claims to lead and which Russia is using for the moment to challenge the West as part of its global strategy. The fact that this demand is unrealistic does not mean that it cannot be appropriated for strategic purposes—quite the contrary. The Russian strategy, which is apparent from a glance at any world map, is to insist on the status quo in Europe—that is, recognition of its own colonial system—while stirring things up in the Middle East and Africa in order to encircle Europe from the south. The freedom and prosperity of the Arab peoples have little to do with Russia's aims. Think of the decimation of the Chechens or the Tartars of Crimea, or the destruction of Arab culture in the formerly Muslim provinces of Daghestan. Russia is simply making use of these imperial dreams to serve its own ends. In any event, these nationalist and imperialist demands are responsible for what is unacceptable in the Arab rebellion, first and foremost the systematic murder of French and Arab civilians, who have been killed indiscriminately simply because they are French or friends of the French.

We are thus faced with an ambiguous demand, the source of which we can approve, along with some of its expressions, but whose excesses are completely unacceptable. The error of the French government since the beginning of the troubles has been its utter failure to make distinctions and therefore to speak clearly, which has licensed the skepticism of the Arab masses and the escalation of the conflict. The result has been to reinforce the extremist and nationalist factions on both sides.

———

The only chance for progress on the issue, now as in the past, is therefore to speak clearly. If the main points are these:

1. Reparations must be made to eight million Arabs who have hitherto lived under a particular form of repression.
2. Some 1,200,000 French natives of Algeria have a right to live in their homeland and cannot be left to the discretion of fanatical rebel leaders.
3. The freedom of the West depends on certain strategic interests.

Then the French government must make it clear that:

1. It is disposed to treat the Arab people of Algeria justly and free them from the colonial system.
2. It will not sacrifice any of the rights of the French of Algeria.
3. It cannot agree to any form of justice for the Arabs that would simply be a prelude to the death of France as a historical actor and an encirclement of the West that would lead to the Kadarization[3] of Europe and isolation of America.

One can therefore imagine a solemn declaration addressed exclusively to the Arab people and their representatives (and note

———

3. The reference is to Janos Kadar, who led Hungary under Soviet domination from 1956 to 1988.—*Trans.*

that since the beginning of the troubles, no French prime minister or governor has directly addressed the Arabs), proclaiming:

1. That the era of colonialism is over. And that while France does not believe itself to be more sinful than other nations shaped and instructed by history, it does acknowledge its past and present errors and state its readiness to repair them.
2. That it nevertheless refuses to give in to violence, especially in the forms it takes today in Algeria. That it refuses in particular to serve the dream of Arab empire at its own expense, at the expense of the European people of Algeria, and, finally, at the expense of world peace.
3. That it therefore proposes a voluntary federal regime in which, under the Lauriol plan,[4] each Arab will obtain the privileges of a free citizen.

Of course, the difficulties will then begin. But there is little chance of their being resolved if this solemn declaration is not made first and directed, I repeat, to the Arab people by every means of transmission available to a great nation. This declaration would surely be heard by the Arab masses, today tired and disoriented, and would also reassure the majority of the French living in Algeria and thus prevent them from blindly opposing indispensable structural reforms.

We turn next to a proposal for resolving the Algerian problem.

4. See below.

27

The New Algeria

As things now stand, it has long seemed to me that the only regime likely to do justice to all segments of the population would be one similar to the Swiss confederation, which embraces several different nationalities. I think, however, that an even more novel system is needed. The Swiss population consists of different groups occupying different regions. Its institutions are designed solely to coordinate political life in the various cantons. By contrast, Algeria is one of the few examples of a country with different populations living together in the same territory. A federation is first of all a union of differences, and what Algeria needs is an association not of different territories but of communities with different identities. Marc Lauriol, a professor of law in Algiers, has proposed a solution to this problem. Even if one does not approve of every last detail of his proposal, it seems to me particularly well adapted to Algerian realities and likely to satisfy the need for both justice and liberty that all the communities of Algeria share.

In essence, Prof. Lauriol's proposal combines the advantages of integration and federalism. While respecting particular differences, it associates both Arab and French populations in the administration of their common interest. To that end, it recommends as a first step a parliamentary reform that would divide the French National Assembly into two sections: a metropolitan section and a Muslim section. The first would include elected officials from metropolitan France and the overseas territories, and the second Muslims living under Islamic law. The rule of proportionality would be strictly respected. One can therefore envisage a parliament of 600 metropolitan deputies, 15 representatives of the French in Algeria, and 100 Muslim deputies. The Muslim section would deliberate separately on all matters pertaining to Muslims alone. The plenary session, combining both French and Muslims, would have jurisdiction over matters of concern to both communities (such as taxes and budget) or to both communities and the metropole (such as national defense). Other questions of interest solely to the metropole (particularly in regard to civil law) would remain exclusively within the competence of the metropolitan section. So laws pertaining only to Muslims would be dealt with solely by Muslim deputies. Laws applicable to all would be decided by all. Laws applicable only to the French would be decided solely by French representatives. In this first phase of the plan, the government would be responsible to each section separately or to both combined, depending on the nature of the question to be decided.

In phase two, after a preliminary period leading to a general reconciliation, the consequences of this innovation would be evaluated. Contrary to all French custom and to firm biases inherited from the French Revolution, the proposal would create two categories of equal but distinct citizens. In this respect, it would constitute a sort of revolution against the regime of centralization and abstract individualism created in 1789, which for many reasons should now be seen as the Old Regime. Prof. Lauriol is nevertheless right to say that his proposal would give rise to nothing less than a federal state in France, an authentic French Commonwealth.[1] Similar institutions could naturally find a place in a system that might eventually be joined by other countries of the Maghreb and black Africa. An Algerian regional assembly would then represent the distinctive views of Algeria, while a federal senate, in which Algeria would be represented, would wield legislative power in regard to matters of interest to the entire federation (such as defense and foreign affairs). It would also elect a federal government responsible to it. It is also important to note that this system is not incompatible with possible new institutions that may emerge in Europe.

That, in any case, should be the French proposal, which would then be maintained until a cease-fire was achieved. At the moment, the intransigence of the FLN has complicated that task. This intransigence is in part spontaneous and unrealistic and in part inspired and cynical. To the extent that it is spontaneous, one can understand it and try to neutralize it with a truly constructive proposal. To the extent that it is inspired, it is unacceptable. Independence is conditioned on a refusal of all negotiation and provocation of the worst excesses. France has no option but to stick to the proposal I described, seek its approval by international opinion and broader and broader segments of the Arab population, and work toward its gradual acceptance.

———

This is as much as one can imagine for the immediate future. Such a solution is not utopian in light of Algerian realities. It is uncertain only because of the state of French political society. Its success depends on:

1. "Le Féderalisme et l'Algérie," *La Fédération,* 9, rue Auber, Paris.

1. A collective will in metropolitan France, and in particular a decision to accept an austerity policy, the brunt of which would have to be borne by the wealthier classes (the working class already bears the weight of a scandalously unjust tax system).

2. A government prepared to reform the Constitution (which in any case was approved only by a minority of the population) and ready and willing to initiate a steadfast, ambitious, long-range policy to establish a French federation.

Objective observers may well feel skeptical that these two conditions can be met. The advent of considerable new human and economic resources in both France and Algeria justifies hopes for renewal, however. If so, then a solution like the one described above has a chance. Otherwise, Algeria will be lost, with terrible consequences for both the Arabs and the French. This is the last warning that can be given by a writer who for the past 20 years has been dedicated to the Algerian cause, before he lapses once again into silence.

Appendix

Indigenous Culture:
The New Mediterranean Culture[1]

I

The Maison de la Culture to which you are being introduced today claims to serve Mediterranean culture. In keeping with the
program of other Maisons de la Culture, it aims to contribute, in
a regional setting, to the promotion of a culture whose existence
and importance are by now well-known. It is perhaps something
of a surprise that left-wing intellectuals are willing to serve a culture that seems of little interest to their cause and that has to
some extent been captured by doctrinaires of the right (such as
Charles Maurras).[2]

To serve the cause of some form of Mediterranean regionalism
might seem to be a throwback to a useless and unpromising variety of traditionalism. Or it might seem to posit the superiority of
one culture over another, standing, say, fascism on its head by

1. Inaugural lecture, Maison de la Culture, February 8, 1937. Pléiade, vol. 1.
2. Charles Maurras (1868–1952), a leader of the nationalist Action Française movement
who supported Mussolini and the Italian fascist takeover of Ethiopia.—*Trans.*

exalting the Latin peoples over the Nordic peoples. This is a source of perpetual misunderstanding. The purpose of this conference is to bring clarity to this question. The error stems from a confusion between Mediterranean and Latin, from ascribing to Rome what began in Athens. For us, it is clear that the only nationalism at issue here is the nationalism of sunshine. We will not subjugate ourselves to tradition or tie our vital future to exploits already dead. A tradition is a past that counterfeits the present. Our Mediterranean is something else: a vibrant region, a realm of joy and smiles. Nationalism has in any case condemned itself by its deeds. In the eyes of history nationalism is always a sign of decadence. Only when the vast edifice of the Roman empire crumbled, when its spiritual unity, from which so many different parts of the world derived the ground of their existence, disintegrated, did nationalities emerge. Since then, the West has never regained its unity. Internationalism is now attempting to restore the Western world's true meaning and vocation. The principle is no longer Christian, however. It is no longer the papal Rome of the Holy Roman Empire. The principle is man. Unity is no longer a matter of faith but rather one of hope. A civilization is durable only to the extent that its unity and grandeur derive from a spiritual principle transcending all nations. India, which is almost as large as Europe but which has no nations or sovereign, has retained its distinct character despite two centuries of English rule.

That is why we reject the principle of Mediterranean nationalism out of hand. The idea of a superior Mediterranean culture is unacceptable. Man expresses himself in harmony with his surroundings, and superiority in the cultural realm depends solely on that harmony. No culture is greater than any other. Some are truer than others. Our only aim is to help this region express itself.

Locally. Nothing more. The real question is whether a new Mediterranean culture is possible.

II. Facts

(a) There is a Mediterranean Sea, which links a dozen countries. The men who bellow in Spain's musical cafés or loiter about the harbor of Genoa or the docks of Marseille, who belong to the hardy, curious breed that inhabits our coasts, are all members of the same family. When you travel in Europe and head south toward Italy or Provence, you breathe a sigh of relief upon encountering the disheveled appearance and robust and vivid customs we all know. I spent two months in Central Europe, in Austria and Germany, wondering why I felt an unaccustomed weight on my shoulders and suffered from a vague anxiety. Recently it dawned on me. The people there were always buttoned up. They could never let themselves go. They did not know the meaning of joy, which is so different from laughter. To make sense of the word "homeland," however, one needs details such as these. A homeland is not an abstraction for which men hasten off to slaughter. It is rather a certain zest for life shared by certain people, as a result of which one feels closer to a Genoan or Majorcan than to a Norman or Alsatian. The Mediterranean is a certain smell, a fragrance that can't be put into words. We feel it in our skin.

(b) There are also facts of a historic nature. Whenever a doctrine has come to the Mediterranean region, in the ensuing clash of ideas it is always the Mediterranean that has remained intact, the region that has conquered the doctrine. Christianity was originally a moving but hermetic teaching, primarily Judaic in character, hostile to compromise, harsh, exclusive, and admirable. Its encounter with the Mediterranean gave rise to something new: Catholicism. A philosophical doctrine was added to the initial emotional aspirations. The monument was adapted to man and thus completed and embellished. The Mediterranean enabled Christianity to enter the world and embark on its miraculous career.

It was also a Mediterranean, Francis of Assisi, who turned Christianity from a religion of inner torment into a hymn to nature and naïve joy. And it was a northerner, Luther, who was responsible for the one attempt to separate Christianity from the world. Protestantism, strictly speaking, is Catholicism wrenched from the Mediterranean and its exalting but dangerous influence.

Let us take a closer look. To anyone who has lived in both Germany and Italy, it is obvious that fascism in these two places is not the same. In Germany its presence is pervasive. One sees it on faces and in the streets. Dresden, a military town, is suffocating beneath an invisible enemy. What you sense first in Italy is the country. What you see on first approaching a German is the Hitlerian, who greets you by saying "Heil Hitler!" In an Italian you see a man who is affable and gay. In this respect, too, the doctrine seems to have receded in the face of the country. By dint of some Mediterranean miracle, people who think humanely are able to live without oppression in a country under inhumane rule.

III

The living reality that is the Mediterranean is nothing new for us, however. For some, the culture of the region is a reflection of Latin antiquity, the antiquity that the Renaissance sought beyond the Middle Ages. It is this Latinity that Maurras and his friends are trying to appropriate. Following the Ethiopian invasion, twenty-four Western intellectuals sought to defend this

Latin order by signing a degrading manifesto extolling Italy's effort to civilize the barbarian African land.

But this is not the Mediterranean to which our Maison de la Culture lays claim, because it is not the true Mediterranean. It is the abstract, conventional Mediterranean symbolized by Rome and the Romans, a people of imitators, which, though it lacked imagination, nevertheless imagined that its martial genius could make up for the artistic genius and zest for life it did not possess. The Roman order that has garnered so much praise was an order imposed by force rather than steeped in intelligence. Even when the Romans copied, they diminished. And what they imitated was not even the essence of Greek genius but rather the fruit of Greek decadence and error. It was not the strong, tough Greece of the great tragedians and comedians but the prettiness and daintiness of the final centuries. What Rome took from Greece was not the life but rather the puerile abstraction and reasoning. The Mediterranean is elsewhere. It is the very negation of Rome and of the Latin genius. It is a vibrant culture, which has nothing to do with abstraction. One can readily assent to Mussolini's claim that he is the worthy successor of the Caesars and Augustuses of antiquity, if by that one means that he, like them, sacrifices truth and grandeur to soulless violence.

What we take from Mediterranean culture is not the taste for reasoning and abstraction but the life—the streams, the cypresses, the bouquets of color. It is Aeschylus, not Euripides, the Doric Apollos, not the copies in the Vatican. It is Spain, with its vigor and pessimism, and not the bluster of Rome. It is landscapes drenched in sun, not the theatrical backdrops in front of which a dictator gets drunk on the sound of his own voice and subjugates the mob. What we want is not the lie that triumphed in Ethiopia but the truth that is being murdered in Spain.

IV

An international zone traversed by many currents, the Mediterranean is perhaps the only region in the world that brings together the great eastern philosophies. It is not a classical and orderly place but a diffuse and turbulent one, like the Arab quarters of many of its cities or the ports of Genoa and Tunisia. The triumphant zest for life, the sense of oppression and boredom, the deserted squares of Spain at noontime, the siesta—that is the true Mediterranean, and it is closer to the East than to the Latin West. North Africa is one of the only regions in which East and West cohabit. At this crossroads, there is no difference between the way in which a Spaniard or Italian lives on the Algerian waterfront and the way Arabs live in the same neighborhoods. What is most essential in the Mediterranean genius may well emerge from this unique encounter of East and West. (On this point, Audisio[3] is the indispensable reference.)

This Mediterranean culture, this Mediterranean truth, exists and is apparent everywhere: (1) linguistic unity: the ease, when one knows one Latin language, of learning another; (2) unity of origin: the prodigious collectivism of the Middle Ages, chivalric orders, religious orders, feudalisms, etc. In all these respects, the Mediterranean offers a concrete image of a vibrant and variegated civilization, impressing its own stamp on all doctrines while accepting new ideas without altering its intrinsic nature.

So why go on?

3. Walter Audisio (1909–1973), an Italian Communist leader.—*Trans.*

V

The point is that a region that has transformed so many doctrines in the past must also transform today's doctrines. A Mediterranean collectivism will be different from a Russian collectivism. The fate of collectivism will not be determined in Russia but in the Mediterranean, and at this very moment in Spain. To be sure, the fate of man has been the issue for a long time now, but the contest may have attained its most tragic form in the Mediterranean. So many resources have been concentrated in our hands. Our ideas will change and adapt. Our adversaries therefore miss the point with their objections. The fate of a doctrine should not be pre-judged, nor should our future be gauged by what has been done in the past, even in Russia.

Our task here and now is to rehabilitate the Mediterranean, to reclaim it from those who have unjustly appropriated it, and lay the groundwork for a new economic order. It is to discover what is real and alive in Mediterranean culture and therefore to encourage its most diverse forms. We are well prepared for this task, especially because we are in direct contact with the East, which has so much to teach us in this regard. We stand here with the Mediterranean against Rome. Cities like Algiers and Barcelona have a crucial role to play, namely, to serve in their own small way those aspects of Mediterranean culture that sustain man rather than oppress him.

VI

The role of the intellectual is difficult right now. It is not his job to change history. Regardless of what people say, revolutions happen first, and ideas come later. It takes great courage today to declare one's faith in the things of the spirit. Such courage is not wasted. Why do intellectuals attract such opprobrium and disapproval? Because people tend to think of them as abstract and argumentative, incapable of taking life as it comes, and giving priority to their own egos over the rest of the world. For those who do not wish to avoid their responsibilities, however, the crucial task is to rehabilitate intelligence by giving it new material to work on. It is to restore the true meaning of spirit by restoring the true meaning of culture, a meaning full of health and sunshine. This courage, I insist, is not wasted, because although it is not the job of intelligence to change history, its proper task is to act on man, who makes his own history. We have something to contribute to this task. We want to restore the link between culture and life. The Mediterranean, which surrounds us with smiles, sun, and sea, teaches us how. Xenophon, in "Retreat of the Ten Thousand," tells us that the Greek army, dying of hunger and thirst after an excursion to Asia marked by repeated failure and humiliation, climbed to the top of a mountain from which the soldiers could see the sea, and they began to dance, forgetting their fatigue and disgust with life. We do not wish to cut ourselves off from life either. There is only one culture: not the culture that feeds on abstraction and geometry, not the culture that condemns, not the culture that justifies the abuse and killing in Ethiopia and legitimates the lust for brutal conquest. We know that culture well and want no part of it. The culture we want lives in the trees, on the hillsides, and in men.

That is why men of the left stand before you today to serve a cause that at first sight might seem to have nothing to do with their political opinions. I hope that by now you are as convinced as we are that the opposite is true. Everything alive is ours. Politics is made for men, not men for politics. Mediterranean men need a

Mediterranean politics. We do not want to live by myths. We live in a world of violence and death, in which there is no room for hope. But perhaps there is room for civilization in the true sense of the word, civilization that places truth above myth, life before dreams. And that civilization has nothing to do with hope. In it, man lives by truths.[4]

The people of the West must back this overall effort. In an international framework, it can be done. If each of us consents to do a modest bit of work in his or her own sphere, country, or province, success is not far away. We know our goal, our limits, and our possibilities. We have only to open our eyes to see what needs to be done: we must make people understand that culture makes sense only when it serves life and that mind cannot be the enemy of man. Just as the Mediterranean sun is the same for everyone, the fruits of human intelligence must be shared by all and not become a source of conflict and murder.

Is a new Mediterranean culture consistent with our social ideal possible? Yes, but it is up to us, and to you, to help bring it about.

4. I am speaking of a new civilization, not of progress within an existing civilization. It would be too risky to play with the dangerous toy known as Progress.

Men Stricken from the Rolls of Humanity

----

57 Prisoners Left Algeria Yesterday
for the Penal Colony

DECEMBER 1, 1938

Le Martinière, commonly known as "the white ship," is actually gray. Long and spacious at 3,871 tons, it seems remarkably empty, because the only cargo in its hold does not take up much room. Actually, it takes up only as much room as has been set aside for it, which is not much.

The ship arrived on Tuesday at 10 o'clock, delayed by a storm in the Atlantic, and wind and rain accompanied its entry into the port of Algiers. On deck were 55 crew members and 41 passengers (guards on their way back to the penal colony). In the hold were 609 prisoners from Saint-Martin-de-Ré.

Moored at the red light, *Le Martinière* bobs up and down on the channel eddies, facing the city, which is barely visible through the veil of rain. The guards lean into the wind as they walk, hands in their leather belts, from which hang large service revolvers. Yet the deck seems deserted, perhaps because of the odor of solitude and despair that hangs about the passageways, where not a soul moves or cracks a joke. But perhaps even more because of the living presence, sinister and hopeless, that one senses beneath the planking.

Nothing can change this feeling, and the cleanliness of the ship, the crispness of the officers' uniforms, and the greetings of the guards struggle in vain to dispel the sense of abandonment that hangs about the windswept decks of this nearly deserted ship. No flotilla of small craft welcomes this vessel with the symphony of foghorns that greets other arrivals.

A Floating Prison

I head for a companionway that leads down into a hold watched by an armed guard. While exchanging a few words with him, I listen to the hoarse, muffled sound that rises intermittently from the depths of the hold, a respiration that is somehow not human. Down there are the prisoners.

When I peer into the hold, all I see is darkness, from which emerge the rungs of the companionway. At the bottom I must stop to allow my eyes to adjust to the darkness. Gradually I am able to make out the reflections from bowls and trays lined up in the middle of the hold, then the gleam of a rifle that advances toward me with another guard, and finally, along the sides of the ship, shiny bars from which hands soon emerge.

The noise I had heard from above has ceased. Now I see that the hold is rectangular, and the bars on each side mark out two cages, each 10 meters long by 5 meters wide.

One of the guards tells me that each of these cages holds between 90 and 100 prisoners. On each side of the ship are four portholes, but they are set very high, and the light they admit illuminates the center of the hold, leaving the prisoners in the shadows, so that it is hard to see their faces.

In the ceiling of each cage is a circular inlet that is attached to a control valve, presently closed. I learn that in case of a riot, each outlet is capable of spewing steam onto the prisoners. At the far end of the hold, between the cages, are two small, stout doors. These give access to two cells barely one square meter each in size, in which prisoners can be placed for punishment.

The ship rolls a bit, so that the light shifts from one cage to the other. One particularly large swell allows me at last to glimpse the prisoners. As the ship rolls, the light abandons them, then returns, only to leave them once again in darkness. It takes me a while to make out human beings in this faceless, breathing, murmuring mass.

Now the light returns, and I look to their faces for signs of resemblance with the world I know. But the night of the hold engulfs them again, and again they are nothing to me but a nameless and troubling shadow.

I head back up the companionway. I do not turn around. I walk the length of the deck and then head down into the rear hold. It is better lit. The cages are smaller. One of them is empty, awaiting the prisoners who will board this afternoon.

In the other cage men sit or hang on the bars. Some are watching me. Some laugh and poke at one another with their elbows, while others stare at me expressionlessly, and still others stare silently at their hands. I see three Arabs hanging from a porthole, trying to catch a glimpse of Algiers. For their comrades, this is a foreign land in what has become a foreign world, but these three, peering through the rain, are still searching for a part of themselves. I am not proud of my presence in this place.

My raincoat is wet, and I know only too well what it brings these men: the smell of a world in which people run free and can feel the wind in their faces. This is the last thing to bring to a place like this. I leave the hold, knowing that there are others, other hands on the bars, other expressionless stares. But I've had enough. As I leave, one of the men asks me in Arabic for a cigarette. I know that it's against the rules. But what a ridiculous response that would be to a man who is simply asking for a sign of fellow-feeling, a human gesture. I do not answer.

The Boarding

I have not yet seen all I came to see, but how can I wait for additional prisoners to board without being overwhelmed by disgust? At noon, I see troops lining up on Amiral-Mouchez wharf, off in the distance. It is raining. Then the skies clear, only to darken again a short while later. The wind and the rain return.

At 2:55, busloads of prisoners and police empty onto the narrow road. No doubt it was unconscious irony that chose three CFRA buses to transport these men, many of whom had probably ridden those same buses in the past. Back then, however, there were stops, and at those stops, one could get off. Today, there is only one stop, at land's end, a few steps from the water's edge, where the departing prisoners' homeland ends.

Brief orders are given. Wasting no time, the guards load the men onto a barge. The rain, which has been falling steadily, now lets up, and a vast rainbow forms in the mist above our heads. Not one of the 57 prisoners crouching in the middle of the barge raises his head. They sit in their coarsely woven uniforms, pull their covers around them, and stare at their duffel bags. The guards surround them, and the barge, towed by a tugboat, shudders as it pulls away from the dock. The rain resumes.

Throughout the crossing, the men keep their heads down. Not one of them looks toward *Le Martinière*. The barge progresses slowly toward the ship as the rain beats down. At 3:10 it pulls up to the aft end of the ship, and the men, watched by rifle-toting guards, climb the ladder to the deck. They are taken to the rear hold and immediately locked up. By 3:30 it is all over. The ship, clasped between the gloomy sea and the rain-swollen sky, makes ready to sail. At 6 P.M., in darkness, *Le Martinière* weighs anchor and disappears, its now illuminated holds filled with its shameful, poignant cargo. I don't know why, but I think of the man who had asked me for a cigarette.

Make no mistake about the meaning of these remarks. I am under no illusion as to how some people will take them. These are "the dregs of society," they will say, and no doubt they are (although one hopes that the people who say this aren't the same ones who think that the elite of society consists of the salon intellectuals who grant themselves the right to judge these dregs).

The point is not to pity these prisoners. Nothing is more abject than the sight of human beings subjected to inhuman conditions. That is the only emotion this piece is meant to convey.

It would have been nice, for instance, not to see elegant women on the dock, drawn there by curiosity. Because curiosity should not have deprived these women of something I am embarrassed to have to remind them of: their sense of decency.

It is not up to us to judge these men. Others have done this for us. Nor is it for us to pity them, which would be childish. The only purpose of this piece is to describe the singular and final fate of these prisoners, who have been stricken from the rolls of humanity. And perhaps it is because this fate cannot be appealed that it is so horrifying.

Letter from Camus to *Le Monde*[5]

JULY 19–20, 1953

To the Editor:

Some of your readers, of whom I am one, may have felt a certain admiration upon learning that after the massacre of July 14, the government filed charges against persons unknown for assaulting officers of the law. This was indeed a rather fine example of cynicism.

When one discovers in addition that most newspapers (not including yours) applied the rather discreet term "disturbance" or "incident" to a minor police operation that cost the lives of seven people and left more than a hundred injured, and when one sees our legislators, in a hurry to get away on vacation, hastily dispatch the embarrassing corpses, one is justified, I think, in asking whether

5. On July 14, 1953, a demonstration organized by the Communist Party ended in violent clashes between the police and about 2,000 Algerian demonstrators on the Place de la Nation. Most of the demonstrators belonged to the Movement pour le Triomphe des Libertés Démocratiques (MTLD), which was calling for the release of Messali Hadj. The killing of 7 demonstrators and wounding of 44 others triggered an intense reaction, echoed by the press. An official investigation concluded that the demonstrators had provoked the police. The incident led to a reorganization of the police intended to exert stricter control on Algerians. See E. Blanchard, "Police judiciaire et pratiques d'exception pendant la guerre d'Algérie," *Vingtième siècle* 90 (2006): 61.

the press, the government, and Parliament would have been quite so nonchalant if the demonstrators had not been North Africans, and whether the police would have fired with such confident abandon if that had been the case. Surely the answer is no, and the victims of July 14 were to some extent the victims of a racism that dares not speak its name.

Nevertheless, one doesn't want to leave the impression that this attitude is shared by all French people, so it also seems to me that at least a few of us, setting partisan motives aside, ought to insist on another investigation, which would focus primarily on those who gave the order to open fire and who, even within the government, have joined that long-standing conspiracy of stupidity, silence, and cruelty that has uprooted Algerian workers, forced them to live in miserable slums, and driven them in desperation to violence in order to kill them on this occasion.

Thank you for your attention.

—Albert Camus

Draft of a Letter to *Encounter*

JUNE 1957

To the Editor:

The Channel is much wider than most people think. Mr. Caracciolo, whose letter can hardly be said to overflow with sympathy for me or my country, can therefore be excused for not knowing that for the past twenty years, first in Algiers itself, quite alone, and later in France, at a time when the public, including that segment of the public which is most vociferous today, systematically ignored Algerian realities, I defended the right of the Arab people to be treated justly. He may be excused as well for not knowing that because of my actions, I was forced to leave Algeria, where I had been deprived of the means of earning a livelihood. It is less excusable, perhaps, given that he was sufficiently interested in my position to have set out to investigate it, that he does not know that one year ago, alone, I am sorry to say, among French writers in Paris with outspoken views on the subject, I went to Algiers to plead for a civil truce in a lecture that was nearly drowned out by the shouts of ultracolonialists calling for my death. This personal effort followed, moreover, a series of articles published in *L'Express,* which summarized my position, and which are available to your correspondent in the offices of that publication. Finally, on March 15, the date of Hungary's national holiday, I publicly expressed the disgust that any free man must feel at the use of torture, whether practiced in Budapest or Algiers.

I hope, but am not certain, that this record of my past service will win me an acquittal by Mr. Caracciolo. I am not certain of this, however, because I know that there are people of a certain cast of mind who would be unwilling to grant an acquittal to men of my sort unless we were to enlist in the Arab guerrilla or accord wholehearted approval to the statements and actions of the FLN. I am unable to grant them this satisfaction, however. Although I am aware that French policy has gone awry, I can still distinguish between Algerian liberty and the fanatical intransigence of over-heated nationalism, dreams of an Arab empire, and above all ter-rorism when it attacks children, women, and innocent civilians, whether Arab or French. No one, after all, can ask me to denounce repression while remaining silent about this terrorism, which is only making Algeria's misfortunes worse. Furthermore, I do not believe—far from it—that Algerian liberty is incompatible with the rights of French settlers in Algeria (1,200,000 of whom have lived in the country for more than a century and 80 percent of whom are people of modest means). The solutions that I have al-ways favored (talks, proclamation of the end of the colonial era, followed by autonomy within a federal framework) are inspired by this historical reality, and they can guarantee the rights and liberties of both populations.

In any case, this reality, which is already quite unlike anything else in history, cannot be compared without rhetorical excess to what is going on in Hungary, where a venerable free nation (de-fended by men who, it should be noted, never made terrorist at-tacks on Russian civilians) has been oppressed and massacred by the troops of a tyrannical foreign power. For such a comparison even to be possible, one of every eight Hungarians would have to be a Russian settler established in the country for a century. I therefore maintain that the abandonment of Hungary by Asian and African nations incapable of distinguishing between the last throes of nineteenth-century colonialism and the rise of a new and powerful colonial empire that is pressuring them in a calculated and relentless fashion is inexcusable and constitutes a serious blow to their own future.

One final word about France. Mr. Caracciolo's letter is by no means indulgent toward my country, and I know that his feelings are shared by many. Please do not expect me to attack my homeland in a foreign publication. I know better than anyone the errors of French policy in Algeria. They are, as I have said elsewhere, vast, tragic, and perhaps irreparable. For the past few months in particular, it has not been easy to be French. In conclusion, however, I would ask your readers to pose themselves a question: Do they know of any other country engaged in a civil as well as foreign war in which a substantial body of public and intellectual opinion has found the strength and generosity to publicly indict the methods employed in that war and, even in the midst of extreme anguish, called for justice to be done to the very people engaged in implacable combat with their own nation?

Sincerely yours,
Albert Camus

Two Letters to René Coty, President of the Fourth Republic[6]

September 26, 1957
Mr. President,

The attorneys for several condemned prisoners in Algeria[7] have sent me the requests for pardon that they recently submitted to you on behalf of their clients. Although I am unable to comment on the substance of these cases, I am moved to add my request to those already before you. My reason for doing so is that these cases do not involve indiscriminate attacks or the repugnant form of terrorism directed against civilian populations, be they French or Muslim. Furthermore, in nearly all of these cases, there were no deaths.

6. Both letters are from Eve Morisi, ed., *Albert Camus contre la peine de mort* (Paris: Gallimard, 2011), 201–4.

7. The Mezzi brothers, Brick Amar, Harfouchi Mohamed ben Ahmed, Haddidi Mohamed, Letabi Rabah, Arabi Rabah, Yanes Bachir, Bourenane, Kab Abderrahmane, Bensaadi Said, etc. According to information gathered by Mostefa Boudina, K. Abderrahmane and M. Bourenane were executed at Serkadji prison in Algiers on October 9, 1957, and Yanes Bachir and Letabi Rabah were executed on October 10. On October 28, 1957, Camus sent another letter to the president, reproduced below. A note of acknowledgment dated October 30 stated that the president "was aware of the delicacy that inspired the terms" of the author's request.—*Trans.*

As an Algeria-born Frenchman whose entire family lives in Algiers and who is aware of the threat that terrorism poses to my own kin as to all the inhabitants of Algeria, the current tragedy affects me daily, and deeply enough that, as a writer and journalist, I have resolved to take no public step that might, despite the best intentions in the world, aggravate rather than improve the situation. Perhaps this voluntary reserve authorizes me, sir, to urge you to use your pardon powers in favor of these condemned men, whose youth or the fact that some have many dependents may deserve your mercy. After lengthy reflection, moreover, I am convinced that your indulgence will ultimately help to preserve the hope of a future for Algeria, which we all share.

Thank you in advance for your consideration.

Respectfully,
Albert Camus

Paris, October 28, 1957
Mr. President,

I have recently received information concerning several more Algerian prisoners who are condemned to death. As in the previous cases, the charges against them do not involve indiscriminate terrorism, and in many instances there were no deaths. I am afraid, however, of presuming on the kindness you recently showed me by reiterating a plea I have already made on several occasions.

I simply ask your permission to state my belief as a French citizen born in Algeria. With the current lull in terrorism and revival of hope for the future, further executions risk jeopardizing this opportunity and spurring new terrorist attacks. By contrast, pardons, visible measures of generosity, would, I am sure, help to calm emotions and foster additional hope. That is why I beg you, sir, to exercise your prerogatives and avoid the worst by suspending executions now.

I am nevertheless aware of the presumptuousness of this new plea and beg you to forgive me for it. If the stakes for our country were not so serious, and if I were not so deeply affected by the Algerian tragedy, rest assured that I would remain in my place and not add to the burdens of your office. I am grateful for your consideration.

Respectfully,
Albert Camus

The Nobel Prize Press
Conference Incident[8]

DECEMBER 14–17, 1957

Stockholm Polemic: Albert Camus Reveals to Swiss Students His Attitude toward the Algerian Problem[9]

Stockholm, December 13. Yesterday afternoon, Albert Camus was the guest of a group of students in Stockholm. During this private meeting, he was asked to respond to a wide variety of questions and once again demonstrated his mastery of language, which is becoming legendary in Sweden. After discussing conscientious objection and the Hungarian problem, Camus himself issued an open invitation: "I have not yet given my opinion about Algeria, but I will do so if you ask me." Various questions were then posed, concerning in particular the freedom of expression of writers and journalists, which several Swedish newspapers have recently questioned. Camus acknowledged the existence of censorship in Algeria, which he seriously regretted, but also insisted on the "total and consoling freedom of the metropolitan press."

8. "Stockholm Polemic," Pléiade, 4:287–90.
9. Article from *Le Monde,* December 14, 1957.

"There is no government pressure in France, but there are influential groups, conformists of the right and left. Believe me when I say with utmost sincerity that no government in the world, if faced with the Algerian problem, would handle it with such relatively minor faults as the French government."

A representative of the FLN in Stockholm then asked Camus why he intervened so readily on behalf of East Europeans but never signed petitions in favor of Algerians. From that point on, the dialogue became confused and degenerated into a fanatical monologue by the representative of the FLN, who pronounced various slogans and accusations, prevented the writer from speaking, and insulted him in the crudest of terms. Camus faced this harsh polemic, which scandalized the Swedish audience, without for a moment losing his poise or dignity. The cause of the FLN, which had previously been disserved on several occasions by the clumsiness and offensiveness of any number of its propagandists, suffered a major moral defeat yesterday in Stockholm, especially since the incident was discussed and disapproved by the local press. In the end, Camus managed to make himself heard, not without difficulty.

"I have never spoken to an Arab or to one of your militants as you have just spoken to me in public. . . . You are in favor of democracy in Algeria, so please be democratic now and let me speak. . . . Let me finish my sentences, because the meaning of a sentence often isn't clear until it ends."

After pointing out that he was the only French journalist forced to leave Algeria for defending the Muslim population, the Nobel laureate added:

"I have kept quiet for a year and eight months, which does not mean that I have ceased to act. I have been and still am a proponent of a just Algeria in which both populations must live in peace and equality. I have said repeatedly that justice must be done to the Algerian people, who must be granted a fully democratic government, and I went on saying this until the hatred on both sides attained such proportions that it became unwise for an intellectual to intervene lest his statements aggravate the terror. It seemed to me that it was better to wait until the moment was right to unite rather than divide. I can assure you, however, that you have comrades who are alive today thanks to actions you know nothing about. It is with a certain reluctance that I explain myself in this way publicly. I have always condemned terror. I must also condemn the blind terrorism that can be seen in the streets of Algiers, for example, which someday might strike my mother or family. I believe in justice, but I will defend my mother before justice."

This declaration was punctuated by ovations.

Letter to the Editor of *Le Monde,* Paris, December 17, 1957

On returning from Sweden, I found in *Le Monde* the articles by your Stockholm correspondent. The statements attributed to me are perfectly correct except for one, which I ask your permission to clarify.

I did not say that our governments had committed only minor faults in dealing with the Algerian problem. I believe the opposite, in fact. But when questioned about the freedom of expression afforded to French writers, I said that it was total. To another question challenging the freedom of our press, I said that the restrictions imposed on that freedom by governments mired in the Algerian tragedy had thus far been relatively minor, which does not mean that I approve of those restrictions, even if they are limited. I have always regretted that there exists no association of journalists that would defend the freedom of the press against the state while enforcing within the profession the duties that such freedom necessarily involves.

I would also like to say, in regard to the young Algerian who questioned me, that I feel closer to him than to many French people who speak about Algeria without knowing it. He knew what he was talking about, and his face reflected not hatred but despair and unhappiness. I share that unhappiness. His face is the face of my country. That is why I was willing to state publicly to that young Algerian, and to him alone, personal explanations that I had previously kept to myself and that your correspondent accurately reported.

—Albert Camus[10]

10. In this article, *Le Monde's* special correspondent in Stockholm, Dominique Birmann, reported some of what Camus said during a debate organized by Swedish students on December 12. It was during this session that Camus, in response to questions from an Algerian student about events then taking place in Algeria, uttered the sentence that (in somewhat distorted form) became famous: "People are now planting bombs in the tramways of Algiers. My mother might be on one of those tramways. If that is justice, then I prefer my mother." Afterward the questions and answers resumed in a lighter tone. But Camus's statement was not passed on to posterity as it was spoken. Birmann ended his article with a paraphrase: "I believe in justice, but I will defend my mother before justice." And of course this "paraphrase" was then widely repeated by various polemicists in yet another version: "Between justice and my mother, I choose my mother."

INDEX

Index